Ruth,

Thanks for all
that you do!

Enjoy

Dr. Tony Watts
#32

# A Face of Courage

The Tommy Watson Story-How did he survive?

*Tommy Watson*

# A Face of Courage

## The Tommy Watson Story-How did he survive?

iUniverse books may be ordered through booksellers or by contacting:

iUniverse
1663 Liberty Drive
Bloomington, IN 47403
www.iuniverse.com
1-800-Authors (1-800-288-4677)

ISBN: 978-0-5955-3056-4 (sc)
ISBN: 978-0-5956-3110-0 (e)

Print information available on the last page.

iUniverse Rev. 09/16/2015

A Face of Courage—The Tommy Watson Story *is a story about courage and perseverance—something we will all need as we go through our daily existence in life. And if you have not yet encountered moments when you have needed these two things, you just keep on living and that day will come. This is a story that deals with many important societal issues—education, self-esteem, male/female relationships, parent/child relationships, race relations, generational gaps, depression, suicide, spirituality, economics, politics, and athletics just to name a few.*

*It is my hope that my story will inspire all readers to discover the best in themselves—and to inspire them to encourage others to do the same. Thanks, and enjoy.*

The events and experiences detailed in this book are all true and have been faithfully rendered according to my recollection. I have changed many of the names in order to protect the integrity and anonymity of individuals involved in these episodes of my life, who have a right to tell their own stories if they choose to do so.

# Chapter I

## *Standing Here Alone—Part One*

I struggled to wake. The cool morning breeze softly soothed my face. Curtains blowing over the partially opened window flashed episodes of sunlight here and there throughout the room, and the smell of fresh bacon sent me a delightful wake-up call with every waving motion of the breeze.

I finally wrestled my eyes open to find I was in terribly unfamiliar territory. I stared at the white walls and high vaulted ceilings; the spring-fresh smell of the blanket clenched in my hands only added more confusion. And there was my little brother Martin lying beside me, still fast asleep. The more I looked around, the more frightened I became.

"Mommy! Daddy!" Surely they would come and rescue me, surely they would.

Seconds later, the hard, wood door of the room burst open. In the doorway stood Grandma Louise in a long, brown robe, her head full of pink rollers. Grandma Louise was my dad's mother.

"It's okay, baby, Grandma's here. Everything going to be all right." She came over to comfort me and wrapped me in her arms. "Don't worry. Grandma's here now, honey."

By this time, Martin, too, had awakened in a panic and needed to be comforted as he wiped the sleep and tears from his eyes. Grandma gathered him in toward us.

"Where's Mommy and Daddy?" I asked.

"They gone away for a little while. You and Martin gonna be staying with me till they get back," she said. "Grandma done cooked y'all some bacon, eggs, grits, and pancakes. Come on and get some of this good eating."

And that was the end of all conversation about Mom and Dad.

Grandma Louise had migrated to Denver, Colorado, in the early sixties from Little Rock, Arkansas, with her children—my dad and his two younger brothers and younger sister. Grandma was from the South. She had worked as a maid for Little Rock families, and then for an affluent Jewish family in South Denver—and that meant she really knew how to "throw down" in the kitchen, much to my little stomach's delight.

The other thing Grandma Louise brought with her from the South was her deep religion. The walls of her apartment were plastered with everything from religious phrases and the Ten Commandments to a picture of a white Jesus and his white disciples. I always found that picture a bit strange; it didn't fit the physical description of Jesus and his disciples in the Bible that was read to us in our Sunday school class.

Martin and I didn't know it at the time, but this was not our first time living with Grandma Louise. The first time had been when Martin and I were even younger. We had been joined in our stay by my two older sisters and older brother, who each had different fathers than Martin and I. After a short stay in a foster home and crisis center, we had all been placed in the custody of Grandma Louise. In the midst of all of the transition in our early lives, somehow my older brother was separated from the four of us and was adopted by another family; because Martin and I were so young, memories of him were left only with my sisters, Melony and Sherl, who were now in foster care somewhere else in the city.

The other thing Martin and I didn't know at the time of our second stay with Grandma Louise was that this was our parents' second time in prison, or "the joint" as some called it. They were there because of their illegal profession as shoplifters, and their chronic use of heroin.

Revealing this type of information was taboo for Grandma Louise, who had grown up in a generation that lived by the unspoken rule: "Whatever problems occur in the house stay only with those who know about them in the house." Besides, this was information that most adults would not have been willing to share with Martin and I, who were only four and five.

I was the older of the two of us. Martin was my shadow, wanting to do everything his big brother did. Because we were so close in age and looked just alike, we were often mistaken for twins, something we would both get tired of hearing as we grew older.

Grandma Louise lived in a corner apartment at 17th and Franklin, which was just on the outskirts of a neighborhood called Five Points, a place that once was called home by America's first self-made female millionaire, Madam C. J. Walker, in 1905. Five Points was Colorado's oldest black neighborhood, and had evolved from its beginnings in the 1800s.

Today, it is home to many of the low- and moderate-income people who live in the inner city of Denver. The neighborhood received its historic name from the five streets that come together in the very center of the community, which also housed many black businesses.

The place where all five streets came together, at 27th and Welton, used to be the hot spot in town for blacks in the 1960s and '70s, a time when there was no longer a need for the banner song, "We Shall Overcome," or for silent marches, or for rigorous hours of prayer. This was the era of the "we have overcome" generation of blacks who had spent most of their school years during the civil rights movement; the new fight was to become the first to win the race of immediate self-gratification. To that end, nightclubs, food joints, and gambling shacks were available throughout the strip that many of the frequenters referred to as simply "The Points."

Many of the black stars and entertainers from that era would come here to perform and hang out at the Rossonna Nightclub, a place where all the pimps and hustlers hung out. This was also the place that captured my dad's attention from the very moment he arrived in the big city from the little country town of Little Rock. The old country boy in him would never be again. Gambling, drinking, using drugs, and chasing women became the forté of this highly achieved high school graduate.

My mother had migrated with her siblings and their mother, my Grandma Mae, to Five Points, too, from Lubbock, Texas. The Points would later become a hangout spot for her as well, which eventually led her to cross paths with Dad.

As the '70s came to an end, Five Points became home to increasing numbers of poor blacks and Hispanics, with a few sprinklings of poor whites here and there. Many of the blacks who had money headed across Colorado Boulevard or "The Boulevard" to Park Hill, where there were beautiful parks and single-family homes. "The Boulevard" became the street that clearly separated the two neighborhoods of Five Points and Park Hill—one side, a home to thriving black families, businesses, and schools; the other, a home to poverty, drugs, and uncontrollable violence.

At Grandma Louise's house, I could often be found in front of the huge window in the dining room, which stretched from floor to ceiling, staring at the flow of traffic and people coming from Colfax Avenue, which was only about a block away. Colfax Avenue was another place that street hustlers, drug addicts, and prostitutes called home. It was a safe place for whites who did not dare to venture into the strip of Five Points.

Colfax was also the dividing line between Five Points and Capitol Hill, which was home to affluent whites. I hated even walking near the neighborhood of those stuffy white folks dressed in their conservative navy blue business suits—those stuffy white folks who always looked at us with hesitation in the stores, who turned up their noses as they hurried out and drove off in a BMW or a Mercedes-Benz.

I sat in front of the window for hours every day, waiting for the moment when the fire trucks would come screaming past the window, bypassing the red yield signal at the corner. It amused me that the fire trucks didn't have to abide by any traffic rules as they came coasting out of the fire station a couple blocks from our apartment. Maybe *I'll be a fireman someday!*

Not long after Martin and I arrived at Grandma Louise's house, we were joined by my dad's baby sister, Aunt Milly, and her daughter Donna, who was the same age as Martin. They came to live with us following Aunt Milly's divorce and the sudden death of her nine-month-old son. It was always difficult for me to suppress the feelings and many questions I had following his death, but somehow I knew any conversation after the funeral would only add to the hurt and pain that Aunt Milly was already experiencing. She always said the one thing that always kept her going was her strong faith. But I had a million questions. *Why did God let babies die? Would I ever see my little cousin again?*

Cleanliness went hand in hand with Grandma Louise. The fresh smell of Pine-Sol swept through the house on a regular basis. The floors were always mopped and swept. The walls stayed nice and white. And it all happened with plenty of help from Donna, Martin, and me. There never seemed to be any dirty dishes or dirty clothes lying around. Despite all Grandma Louise's hard work around the house, however, the three of us did manage to keep the dining room flooded with baby dolls and football helmets.

Going to church was mandatory in Grandma Louise's house. We were in church with Aunt Milly every Wednesday night, Friday night, Saturday afternoon (for kid's choir rehearsal), and on Sundays for what seemed to be most of the day. I loved being in the kid's choir.

The church we attended was called The House of Joy, and that it was—a hand-clapping, foot-stomping, gum-popping, head-swaying, body-shaking, tongue-shouting, leg-jerking, body-stumbling church in the neighborhood of Park Hill, which was about the only thing that brought us to that side of town. It seemed as if everyone who attended the church had a nice big expensive car, and wore nice suits and big colorful hats to match their glamorous dresses; at least, that was my observation from the church van that brought us to church because we didn't have a car.

Blacks streamed in from all across the neighborhood, parking their cars blocks away to attend a Sunday service that always sounded like a big party. The kids usually had their own service in the church basement, right beneath the floor-shaking adult service. After church, we kids always got a kick out of seeing the end results of a wild-spirited adult service: the sanctuary looked and smelled like a hot, sweaty sauna, and the adults left with wrinkled garments, saggy Afros, and fluffed out Jeri curls.

On the days when children's church was closed, all the kids attended service with the adults. Attending these services, I grew accustomed to two things. First, Martin, Donna, and I always got smashed back against the hard, brown pews when Aunt Milly started shouting and praising the Lord; the slightest song from the choir or message from the preacher would send Aunt Milly into what looked like convulsions. First her head would start swaying back and forth, and then she would begin to speak in tongues. Suddenly, she would be hollering and jumping all over the place, and we always ended up smashed into the wooden pews beneath her. I was always embarrassed to have the whole church watching as the ushers pulled her up off us.

The other thing I could always count on was receiving those painful "wake yo' butt up" pinches. No matter how long the service lasted, we were expected to at least give the appearance of being attentive. Any adult who caught us playing or dozing off would give us "the pinch"— a twist and pull that often broke the skin—followed by the words, "Wake yo' butt up," or "Stop messing around." It amazed me how many of those same adults who found fault with Donna, Martin, and me couldn't seem to control their own unruly children.

If there was anything that caught and kept my attention during church, it was thinking about Grandma Louise's Sunday dinners. She never attended church with us, but, rather, had a nice dinner prepared each Sunday when we came through the door after church. She felt that many of today's Christians were a bunch of hypocrites. Nevertheless, when we got home we were greeted with the smell of hot buttermilk biscuits, cornbread, ham hocks, neck bones, candied yams, and warm gravy that I slopped across the tender fried pork chops. A sweet potato pie with homemade crust would finish things off. If someone prepared a good meal, Grandma Louise used to say, "They put their foot in it." Well, in Grandma Louise's case, she put her foot, elbow, hand, knee, fingers, ankle, and leg into everything she cooked.

In addition to loving food, I always had an ear for good music and enjoyed dancing, despite never really being a good dancer. Every Saturday morning, while cleaning, we listened to the gospel hour on radio station 1510 kdko. Whenever a song came on that I liked, I'd start my routine—a slow winding of my hips in a circular motion. And, as the music continued, so did I. Faster and faster I went, winding my hips until finally everyone in the room erupted in laughter. I mean almost everyone but Grandma Louise and her sister Aunt Mary, who could do nothing but shake their heads in disgust. "There that boy go again, Louise, doing that ole nasty dance," Aunt Mary would say, showing stern disapproval.

Despite my obsession with "nasty dancing," I managed to stay dedicated to the children's choir. This involvement in the choir later led to an opportunity to make a recording of our favorite church song, "Peanut Butter and Jelly." Thumbing through a case of 45-rpm records and seeing my own song always gave me great joy. After months of preparation, the day of the recording session finally came. The journey to the recording studio called for a long ride through many unfamiliar suburban neighborhoods, but I didn't mind; I was running on pure adrenaline. The fifteen-passenger church van took us through foreign-looking neighborhoods with big yards and fancy cars. Farther and farther from Five Points we traveled, until, finally, we arrived at the studio.

Martin, Donna, and I scrambled out of the van in a mad dash behind the older kids, who had bolted out and into the studio. It was time to go to work.

"Okay, everyone, take your places," the choir director said as she settled us in the studio, leaving to watch and listen from the monitor in the other room. Martin, Donna, and I were bumped to the back of the tightly occupied room by some of the older kids, who just so happened to be the choir director's kids, nieces, and nephews. Offering little resistance, we took our places in the back beneath the microphone that hung from the ceiling.

After being given our three-second lead-in count by the director over the overhead speaker, we launched into our song. "I don't want no peanut butter and jelly …," we sang with great pride and joy. "I don't want no peanut butter and jelly …"

And, in an instant, we were abruptly interrupted by the director, who came back into the room. "That is not the way we practiced this song. Now let's get this thing right, because we don't have a lot of time," she said, exiting the room.

"All right. Once again from the top," she instructed from the overhead speaker.

We began again, Martin, Donna and I singing at the top of our lungs, trying to keep pace and avoid being drowned out by the older kids. "I don't want no peanut butter and jelly ...," we continued to shout. "I don't want no peanut butter and jelly ..."

Again we were cut off by the director, who came storming back into the room. She scanned the room looking for the weakest link, and giving us a look that said, "Y'all better get this thing right."

And, just as before, we were given the cue to start. Again, the three of us joined in just the way we had practiced the song a hundred times before, singing out at the top of our lungs, "I don't want no peanut butter and jelly ... I don't want no peanut butter and jelly ..."

No sooner did we get to the end of the first verse, than the director came storming in again. Now what? By now, the eyes of the older choir members had become a bit shifty as they looked for someone to blame for the disharmony. This is going to be a long night. After a few minutes of shouting instructions and rearranging some of the older kids, the director left and we were given instructions from the sound booth to begin again.

The frown on our director's face was a sure sign that she was about to reach her boiling point. No one wanted to see her reach that point, so we started again, singing just as we had sung in the past, but with even more "oomph"—"I don't want no peanut butter and jelly... I don't want no peanut butter and jelly ..."

Once more, the director stormed into the room, this time with her shoes and earrings off; she looked like a woman ready for battle. Many of the heads in front were clearly turned facing the three of us, implying that one of us was the problem. What do ya'll know?

But it didn't matter what anyone else thought, her opinion was all that counted. So, on that last occasion when she left the room, she did not leave alone. She took someone with her. That someone was me, led out of the room by my shirt, with my head down. I couldn't believe it. "But I worked so hard for this opportunity," I wanted to protest.

I spent the rest of my time at the studio watching from the monitor as the choir went on to record "Peanut Butter and Jelly" without me. Being taken from that room took away my opportunity to debut on an album—and all my dreams of becoming a singer as well. As I listened to the choir, each verse, each word, each note tore at my soul. I had failed. I sat next to the cheering adults quietly sobbing and not being consoled. My zeal for singing was gone.

This crushing moment left me with only my other childhood dream—to grow up and play for the Denver Broncos—which today seems a bit ironic. Given the fact that this was a team of players who very seldom, if ever, came out to visit with kids in my neighborhood, even though it was a team that had many black players who had come from similar environments. With no males in our household to introduce me to this dream, it would remain just that—a dream.

It was a dark autumn night as Martin, Grandma Louise, and I trod through the dry fallen leaves in our final stretch home from Burger King. The sounds of the leaves crunching beneath our feet bounced like music off the fancy marble walls of the bank, creating an echo effect as we walked past. The bank lay dormant, as everyone had deserted the premises for the evening. Quietness swept over the streets. The music of our stepping and crunching in unison was like the sound of a mesmerizing jazz song.

Then, suddenly, in an instant, our musical melody was interrupted by a streaking shadow. Grandma Louise was knocked to the ground. "Oh! No! He snatched my pocket book!" she yelled.

He *did what?* Furious, I took off in pursuit of the assailant, hoping to get close enough to deliver a nice swift kick to his shins and recover Grandma's purse. My careless rage had me shouting at the fleeing coward all throughout the quiet streets. Finally, it became obvious that I was not going to catch the adult villain, who had taken flight through the alley. My heart was throbbing. Sweat dripped from my chin. I stood, slowed with fury, fists clinched. It was a tough decision to terminate the chase.

With my last step, I turned around to see Grandma's face frozen in total disbelief. The disbelief seemed to have less to do with her purse being stolen and more to do with the screams of profanity that had come from my five-year-old mouth during my short pursuit.

"Boy, who in the world taught you to say words like that?" she asked me.

It wasn't long after this event that Sherl, Melony, Martin, and I were back with Mom and Dad, living in a rundown apartment building that sat at the corner of 26th and Ogden in the heart of Five Points. Our new place was quite different from Grandma Louise's home; many of our days were spent trying to exterminate the army of cockroaches that moved like wildfire through our three-bedroom apartment.

"Damn! That sucker got away again," Dad shouted, while inspecting the mousetraps he had spread strategically beneath the stove, refrigerator, and sink and in every corner of every room. The days of waking up to the smell of bacon, eggs, and pancakes at Grandma Louise's were over. Now there was a morning scramble out of bed to be one of the first to get the last divides of milk for the Captain Crunch cereal. And when you were not lucky enough, the alternative was cereal and faucet water. Yuk!

Even the way Mom and Dad decorated the apartment made this place different from Grandma Louise's place. Pictures of blacks and other cool art covered every inch of our walls. My favorite was a painted picture of twelve dogs sitting in a pool hall, drinking beer and playing pool, while a seductive female poodle sat at the end of the pool table showing the male dogs a little leg as an incentive for winning. Seeing this painting every morning when I rose always made me giggle.

The other picture that I found fascinating was the painting of an exotic Nubian queen standing with her hands on her hips, smoking a cigarette with her beautifully shaped Afro and her breast fully exposed to every passing eye. Man, how I wanted a girlfriend one day who would look just like that, cigarette and all.

The smell of incense filled our small living room, which was always strewn with flamboyant record albums of old-school artists. Curtis Mayfield, The Ohio Players, The Gap Band, The Commodores, The O'Jays, Earth, Wind & Fire, The Jackson Five, The Temptations, and, my favorite, Marvin Gaye, blared from our record player throughout the apartment complex.

My excitement to be with Mom and Dad outweighed my yearning to ask where they had been during the time we were with Grandma Louise. And, just like at Grandma Louise's house, neither of them spoke a word of it. Life went on.

In my new school, there were not many days that passed when I didn't hear one of my classmates talking about how they lived with only their mom and how they wished their dad was around.

"Man, my dad was supposed to come by this weekend, but he never showed up," was the common complaint many of them shared. I felt like the luckiest kid in the world to be able to say, "Well, my dad lives with me." Hearing these stories gave me a deeper appreciation for my dad and the time we spent together.

Often, when I was not in school, I could be found tagging behind Dad at Green's Gambling Shack, listening through a haze of cigarette and cigar smoke to the old blues songs blaring from the jukebox. I got a chance to hear and see him and his buddies talk big stuff and lose big money.

"Nah, one mo' hand," a drunk loser would yell out to Mr. Green, who sat at the end of the table wearing a folded down gray hat, chewing on an inch of cigar, and holding a bat, which sometimes came in handy against the unruly.

"Man, you already done lost all yo' money. Now it's time to go home," Mr. Green would insist, shoving the drunken card player out the back door. The theme song for most of the drunken losers when they got kicked out of Mr. Green's was that of a classic blues song by BB King, "The Thrill is Gone." Oh how macho such a place seemed to be to my young mind.

But it wouldn't be long before changes in our household would challenge my newfound fondness for Dad. One night I awoke to horrifying screams and pleading. "No, no! Please … don't hit me any more …"

"Martin, you hear that?" I said, shaking him awake. "We got to get Melony and Sherl."

By the time we got to the hallway, both Melony and Sherl were already there, trying to peer through the darkness to see where the screams and commotion were coming from.

We tiptoed down the hallway hand in hand to discover that the commotion was coming from Mom and Dad's room. Through the door we heard the blows as Dad's fist connected with Mom's frail body. Her fading voice by now was only able to whisper, "No more, please! No more."

The sound of each blow that penetrated through the door and into my ears created a fire of rage in me that would burn for what seemed like an eternity.

The shouting and cursing stopped later that night, but the screams of Mom getting beaten merciless by Dad never ceased in my mind and reduced my enthusiasm for him to lukewarm. *How could any man beat a woman like that?*

Though the violence was severe and occurred often, none of us dared to call the police—not through any of the terrifying, violent-filled nights that followed. I believed that the police in my neighborhood were as dangerous as the perpetrators. I had bore witness from my window one night to a couple of "boys in blue" unleashing their wrath on a helpless drunk in our alley.

Awakening to this type of madness was painful and was like awakening to an alarm clock sounding off prematurely. Many nights I woke up in a cold sweat. "Man, there they go again," Martin and I would agonizingly express to one another.

As time went on, I began to anticipate the violence, lying down each night trying to get mentally prepared for the battles. I would spend hours tossing and turning, not wanting to fully give into the darkness and torment of the night.

What always made the violence-filled nights even more difficult to comprehend for me were the nonchalant faces Mom and Dad masked themselves with each following morning. Even at the tender age of six, I wanted to know what was wrong in Mom and Dad's relationship so I could fix it for them. The last thing I wanted was to be fatherless like many of my classmates at school. What can I do to help?

It didn't take long for the drama at home to start affecting my behavior and attitude in school. I started to become withdrawn, and I hated school. In many ways, my situation at home was starting to sound like that of many of the other students. My dad was present, but many of us were children who were growing up before our time. Flying off the handle on my teachers and classmates seemed to ease the pain that I was feeling inside, and I started to lose ground academically as a result. "I don't have to do a damn thing," were the words that I adopted when I did not want to do work in the classroom.

"Well, I guess you will have to do it later," my teacher would say, never following up on her promises.

It would be Mom's younger brother J.R. who would bring a temporary end to the beatings.

Uncle J.R. was athletic and strong and twice the size of Dad. Women all over town fainted to be in his presence, but his true and only love was his older sister, my mom, Fae. She had looked after him when Grandma Mae turned to alcohol to cope with the pain of losing my grandfather, whom I never knew. Mom and J.R. and their siblings had bounced in and out of foster homes and, as a teenager, J.R. had even lived in an abandoned car for a while until Mom rescued him. I welcomed his presence in our house.

"Man, I'll kill you if you ever put yo' hands on my sister again," Uncle J.R. yelled in his many unsuccessful attempts to catch Dad, who would flee out of the house through whatever window or door was nearest. "Fae, I don't know why you stay with that no-good bastard," he adamantly expressed, heading out the door, mad at Mom for staying with Dad.

Regardless of his strong disapproval of Mom's relationship with Dad, J.R. was always ready and willing when the next call came for his assistance. *And so life goes on.*

Bullies were also a big part of the lifestyle among the kids in our apartment complex. Bullies roamed the floors of the complex every day seeking out the blood of the weak. If they couldn't find any victims there, their journey usually brought them to the park across the street where many of us played and sought peace from the chaotic environments of home.

One day, while Martin and I were playing on the merry-go-round, Richard, one of the lead henchman in the club of bullies, approached Martin out of the blue and let him have it right smack in Martin's stomach. Wham! Immediately, I began to scan the area for Melony and Sherl, our playground protectors. *Damn, they're nowhere in sight,* I thought to myself, knowing what the possible action was before me.

Mom and Dad had always emphasized that, if one of us got into a fight, we'd all better be in that same fight—win or lose—or face serious consequences. A whipping when we got home was the last thing any of us wanted to face. But Richard was older than I, and twice my size.

With this dilemma hanging over my head and Martin on the ground on all fours crying, I thought it would behoove me to at least give Martin some backup. And so I took off running towards Richard in a half-hearted effort, hoping to land a few body shots. I was swinging and kicking like a wild man. *Take that, punk!*

Suddenly, in what seemed like a nanosecond, he delivered two serious hits. I lay doubled over on the ground; so much for that fight. Now I, too, had fallen to the mighty hands of Richard.

"You little punks want some more of me?" he shouted at the two of us, as we looked at each other fearfully not knowing how or if we should respond.

So we decided to do what most kids do when they are in trouble or in need of help on the playground—they flee home and get Mom and Dad, which is exactly what Martin and I did with no hesitation.

"Mom, Dad! That boy over there …," both of us yelled as we scrambled through the front door, trying to give our version of what had just happened, including my vain attempt to fight back, hoping to get some parental reinforcement.

"… and I hit him in the stomach," Martin lied while gasping for air.

"Yeah, I kicked him …," I hyperbolized.

But the looks on Mom and Dad's faces said it all. It wasn't enough of an attempt. Our exaggerated story of the "shock and awe" campaign that we had bestowed on Richard had failed. We had to go back and face the bully in round two. As parents, they knew that, if we continued to run from Richard every day, we would never be able to set foot on the playground again. And, with that, we were led back out the front door and told, "Go back and do what y'all need to do." The battle for playground peace was on. But this time we were not going empty handed. I pulled the belt from my shorts.

When we arrived back at the playground, Richard was already in pursuit of more victims. He stood throwing rocks at another group of kids who were hiding behind a giant slide in the middle of the playground. Slowly, we crept behind a bush a few feet from Richard, looking for the opportunity to jump out and give him some payback.

Finally, the opportunity presented itself, and, when Richard bent down for more ammunition, I dashed at him and delivered a blow across his back with my belt buckle. Martin came in from the other side delivering kicks and punches. Things were looking pretty good for the new kids on the block in our stand against the playground bully. *Take that, punk! You better not ever mess with my little brother and me ever again!*

But, in that instant, just as before in round one, the script flipped, and Richard had my belt in his hand and was in hot pursuit of Martin and me as we headed for the hills trying to get some serious parental rescuing. In our long sprint home, it became very apparent to me that Richard was a kid to whom whippings were not foreign—probably from the receiving end, and definitely on the delivering end. Had I not known better, I would have thought it was my dad whipping the two of us; we both took hits all the way up to our front door, at which point Mom and Dad finally chased Richard off.

Mom and Dad could do nothing but laugh at what they had just witnessed. The sight of their sons being chased down the street hollering for help and getting whipped with the belt that was supposed to protect them must have been pretty amusing. Ha ha!

Despite the end result of this grudge match, we learned just how important it was to stick together through thick and thin. We also learned the ever-so-important lesson that sometimes it takes war to get peace. Ironically, we never had any more trouble out of Richard after that day.

Shortly after our confrontation with Richard, we moved into a three-bedroom, single-family house on 22nd and California Street, where we also found ourselves in a new school. Mom and Dad never said why the sudden move was necessary, but I figured it had to do with the fact that our family had just expanded with the birth of my baby sister Carmen. Be that as it may, things were starting to look better for us. What really made me believe that we were headed in a new direction was the additional arrival of our family dog Sheba. From what I had been able to gather from families on television, having a family dog equaled prosperity and advancement.

Our home still rested in Five Points, but on the other side, near downtown. Inside, the rooms were dark and gloomy, and outside the balding lawn boasted patches of weeds here and there. But, whatever the case, 22nd and California was our new home.

In school, it didn't take long to discover that being in a new setting with new kids didn't necessarily mean new and different social challenges. In fact, the words coming from the lips of my classmates on the playground during recess at Ebert Elementary reflected the same yearning the kids had had at my former school, Gilpin Elementary. There was an ongoing yearning for a daddy—any daddy—to come around and spend time with them. What would life be like if Daddy came around?

Our seven or so months together on 22nd and California had been the best time we had ever spent together as a family. The fighting between Mom and Dad had diminished greatly. *Wow, this feels great!* It almost seemed to be too good to be true. And, in fact, it was too good to last.

"I need to talk with yall's momma and daddy. I need my money," our landlord Mr. Mack angrily said to Melony and Sherl, who stood guarding the entry way into the house one day while Mom and Dad hid behind the door.

"They're not here, they ah, ah ... went to the store," Melony responded, just as she had been coached by Mom and Dad.

"Well, you tell them they're late on the rent again and I need my money in a week or else." Mr. Mack concluded, skeptically walking back to his dirty blue pickup truck.

"You make sure you tell them. They have until next week," he yelled out the window over the sound of his loud, whistling muffler.

Up to this point, I had never thought about—nor had the family ever talked about—where Mom and Dad got the money to take care of us. The only thing they ever said to us about money, whenever we asked for some, was, "Money don't grow on trees" We never got an explanation of the source of the money in our household. Despite not having this answer to this question, the only thing that I could do was to be thankful for what we had. All I knew was that I had a roof over my head and clothes on my back. Thank God. So I thought.

But that was about to change, and change drastically. In the weeks that followed, we were kicked out of our place on 22nd and California. Our travels landed us briefly with a friend of the family, and then at the first of three motel rooms in which we would reside in over the next several months.

The Colonial Motel was a cheap, dingy-looking motel that sat beneath the overpass of Interstate 70, miles from our previous home and school, which we still attended whenever possible. I was so disappointed in Mom and Dad, but I dared not utter a word.

Martin and I slept in one bed, and Melony, Sherl, and Carmen slept in the other bed beside ours. Mom and Dad slept on the floor in our one-room dungeon. I cried myself to sleep nearly every night, hoping to withstand my frustration. *How did this happen? Why did all of this have to happen to my family?*

Mom and Dad gave no explanation for the change in our conditions, and their silence sometimes hurt more than the abrupt transition. I just wanted some assurance that things were going to get better. "Well, kids, we have just momentarily fallen into some tough times, but your momma and I are working hard to try to get a house," were the words that the responsible, loving dad always shared on television with his family during tough times. And, just like on television, I yearned to hear those same words from Dad, but they never came. Life went on.

Living in smaller quarters meant other sacrifices also had to be made. Sheba had been left behind—man, how I missed faithful old Sheba. We left many of our clothes behind, and the ones we had were no longer clean and neatly folded in drawers, but were dirty, and wrapped in bundles of sheets in the corner. Each day I arose to put on the same clothes I'd already worn for days. *Why? Why does the dirty shirt with the black ring around the collar and musty armpits have to be resting on my back? Why are these socks that were once white, and are now smelly, brown and itchy, cling to my feet? Why am I wearing these pants that I have outgrown—these pants that now conclude in the middle of my shins exposing the gray ash of my legs to the world? Why all the painful remarks and laughter in school from my classmates? Why? Why? Why?*

Mom and Dad were also feeling the same pain and frustration that were brewing in me. Their ugly arguments and fights from the past started to resurface. Not having access to J.R. any more meant we had no choice but to endure and try to ignore Dad slapping Mom around in front of us.

With all this anger built up inside of me, school continued to become the place for me to unleash my wrath. If my teacher or classmates said anything to me I didn't like, they heard from me, "Kiss my ass, and, if you don't like that, I will kick your ass." It became an all-day, every-day slogan for me. In today's school system I would have certainly been labeled as defiant or perhaps even perceived as a child with an emotional behavior disorder. Or I might have been doped up with Ritalin, despite the fact that much of my difficult behavior was attributed to a painful and challenging home life that did not seem to be getting better.

The one time that always brought my classmates and me together for fun was recess. On the playground one afternoon, one of the kids yelled out, "Hey, let's throw rocks at the drunks across the street at the park." With those words, we all hopped up and scrambled through the playground searching for ammunition to throw over the six-foot-high fence that caged us within the boundaries of the school. I couldn't wait to unleash my wrath onto the hopeless drunks. The drunks in my neighborhood were considered winos. These were the folks who had surpassed the arena of alcoholics years ago and now made drinking cheap liquor a way of daily life each and every moment of the day. *At least alcoholics have jobs and families, these low-life drunks have neither.*

"Let's get them lowlifes," another yelled in our sprint to do battle. After gathering the last of the sharp-edged rocks we could find on the playground, we were ready for war.

"Let's do this," we all yelled in excitement, arriving to the fence to take aim.

"Ready, aim, fire!" Carlos, our class troublemaker, instructed.

As I cocked back to throw my sharp-edged rock, I experienced a heart-dropping discovery. As I looked at the faces of the "low-life drunks," my world was shook up. *Oh, no! I can't believe it.* The drunks who were about to be on the receiving end of our mayhem were familiar—they were my Grandma Mae and her friends. I couldn't believe it.

*What should I do?* With tears in my eyes, I continued looking at Grandma Mae as she stumbled through the park with the rest of the drunken winos. Slowly, I dropped the rocks I had gathered and held in my shirt and walked away as quietly as I could. I hoped no one would notice my retreat, especially Grandma Mae. Torn between further ridicule from my schoolmates and defending the humanity of my grandmother and her friends, I continued walking, head down and eyes low. My tears began to flow even harder when I heard the laughter of the rock throwers as they basked in the glory of claiming whose rocks hit which winos.

"Did you see that? My rock cracked that one over there in the head!"

"Aw, man, that ain't nothing—mine hit that one over there in the face!" I hoped desperately that Grandma Mae had not been on the receiving end.

Not responding, not doing what was right, not defending my grandmother, was a heavy burden that I would carry with me for some time.

Meanwhile, at home we were eating less and starting to see less and less of Mom and Dad, who would often return home in the wee hours of the morning with food from Church's Chicken or cinnamon rolls and milk for us. Mom and Dad's new behavior patterns were tied directly to the full-blown indulgence of their heroin addiction, something we were unaware of at the time. Nevertheless, we would scramble out of bed, still half asleep, to eat as much as our empty stomachs could handle before trying to retrieve a few more hours of sleep before school the next day. This would be a pattern that would go on for sometime. *Is life going to get any better?*

"Hey, Fuji," Dad yelled out to the foreign motel owner one day, who was watering the dirt in the parking lot in an attempt to keep the dust storms to a minimum. "Hey, Fuji," he yelled a second time. Our key was not working and we couldn't get into our motel room. "God damned Fuji, I know you hear me."

Finally he responded. "I want you and you family off me property now," the motel owner said in a foreign accent, walking toward us. "I had enough of you people."

In an instant, a hostile bickering match between him and Dad ensued. At times it even seemed as though the two of them were going to break out in a scuffle.

Back and forth they went. It was difficult to decode some of the words coming from the foreigner's mouth, but the root of the problem became obvious when he said, "You not paid rent in weeks, you must go before I call police." There was no doubt about it; we were not getting back into the motel room. Everything in the room had to stay—as ransom for the neglected payments. *What does all this mean? He has to be joking about us having to leave and not being able to get any of our stuff from the room, right?*

Unfortunately, it was not a joke, but our new lifestyle reality.

The owner was serious as serious could get. And, before long, we were forced to give in to his unwavering demand to leave the premises. I couldn't believe it. I longed to cry, but I knew it would do no good. I stumbled back to the car, led along by Mom, who held on to the end of my arm. We were leaving behind every possession that we owned, including my most cherished possession, snakeskin cowboy boots that Mom and Dad had just given me. We were left with literally nothing but the clothes on our backs. How will we survive? This was the question that I wanted answered. However, my beat-up emotions and the sad faces of my siblings said it all—this was real-life survival.

In the weeks that followed, we spent each day not knowing where or with whom we would rest our heads at night. We stayed in the homes of friends and in several other motels before finally landing at our new place on 38th and Williams.

Being in our own place provided some relief. I, however, was not going to let my guard down and was only cautiously optimistic about our future with Mom and Dad.

Slowly, I was starting to discover that the mighty concept of "time" could change a person's perspective on life, but time alone could never wash away the depths of internal pain of individuals who had been wounded emotionally. In addition to this, I was also learning how to better suppress my feelings and hide them from the rest of the world. And so life went on.

Finally, after months in our new place, my siblings and I started to breathe a little easier, with the exception of Carmen, whose innocent heart and mind at a little more than one year of age were oblivious to our situation. Despite what we were feeling, the behavior of Mom and Dad remained the same.

After a long year in first grade that involved a lot of missed classes and failed assignments, I somehow managed to pass and move on to second grade. With Melony, Martin, Sherl, and me still attending Ebert Elementary, we had to become creative in finding transportation for our several-mile journey to school. This was a task of great difficulty. "How will we get to school today?" was the question of the morning. We walked, caught the city bus, and even stole bikes from the neighborhood to get ourselves to school during the many days when Mom and Dad weren't around.

On the days when we couldn't find Grandma Mae to baby sit Carmen, Melony opted to stay home from her sixth-grade class with her.

"I'm the oldest, and it's my responsibility to take care of y'all when Mom and Dad aren't here, so y'all go on to school and I'll stay with Carmen," she'd say, pushing us out the door. "Go on. I will see you all when you get home."

And more and more we continued to see less and less of Mom and Dad, with the exception of the first of the month, the day our welfare check came—a check that we never saw any part of.

It was becoming the norm for our parents to be gone for days at a time without checking up on us. Nearly all our clothes came from the second-hand clothing shelf from the church around the corner through vouchers they gave to Grandma Mae. This clothing provided another opportunity for the kids at school to make fun of us. It didn't take a rocket scientist to figure out that our gear had had previous owners when we walked into the school wearing shirts bearing the names of individuals and events with whom we had no connection. "Welcome to the Hernandez Family Reunion" and "Lisa and Mike Forever," a couple of my most-often-worn shirts read. I tried to buoy myself up. Things have to start getting better for us at some point.

Food was also becoming scarcer at home each day. Some days it seemed as if we were going to literally starve to death as we sat waiting and hoping for Mom and Dad to return with food—something that usually didn't happen. To that end, we learned how to become scavengers in our world. When we weren't gobbling down meals at school, much of our days were spent shuffling through the empty cabinets at home for food for ourselves and Carmen, who we were basically raising. A mayonnaise and sugar sandwich was now like a five-star meal.

Things had become so bad that, after returning in tears from our house one day, Grandma Louise told Aunt Milly that she was going to take custody of all of us. She had found us searching through our garbage and sink for food.

"Okay, Martin, you stay here with Carmen while we go make our run," Melony instructed before she, Sherl, and I headed out into the neighborhood grocery stores to steal cupcakes, cereal, soda, crackers, candy, and anything else we could fit into our pockets that would allow us to survive another day. At times, it almost seemed as if the store clerks felt our pain; often they made little or no attempt to stop us from entering the store and then running out the emergency exit with the stolen goods.

"Come back here, you little bastards," many of them often times yelled from the doorway, but gave no attempt to exit the premises of the store and follow us.

Over fences and down the allies we would run tirelessly until our arrival to the living room floor, to evenly divide the goods.

As badly as we wanted to, we never complained to Mom and Dad. We had been raised by the law, "Thou shalt honor thy father and thy mother." This was an ancient gospel law that I often felt should have been extended: "Mothers and fathers shalt honor and support thy children." I left this only as a commentary in my mind, and life went on.

"I'll tell y'all what, if y'all can have Carmen walking by the time we get back, me and ya' mamma will take y'all roller-skating," Dad said one afternoon, heading out the door with Mom and carrying two garbage bags full of "merchandise," as they called it, draped over his shoulder.

With a marvelous deal like this, nothing else needed to be said. Immediately, we began setting up our training course in the living room.

"Hurry! Move that couch over there and move the other one right here," Melony ordered Martin and me. The two couches, setting on opposite sides of the room, would now become destination points for Carmen.

"Let's do it!" We chanted with great excitement and anticipation of roller-skating.

In no time, we were going at it, getting Carmen's training underway. Back and forth we crawled from one couch to the other, guiding Carmen by the arms and looking for any signs of independent balance. Minute after minute, hour after hour, we treaded the hardwood floor on our knees, fighting off exhaustion with the thought of being able to finally go roller-skating with the other kids from the neighborhood.

"Walk to big brother," I prompted her from a few steps away. "Come on, Carmen, you can do it!" Back and forth for several more hours we went, taking only a very short break or two.

Finally! Sure enough, by the end of the day, all we had done had paid off. Carmen was walking! We all celebrated, skipping across the squeaky floors. The thought of being able to go roller-skating with the other kids couldn't escape my mind. Butterfly sensations rumbled through my stomach, and chills rolled down my back in my anticipation of our reward. I couldn't wait to try to be the first one to scramble to the door and tell Mom and Dad the good news.

And so that evening we all camped out like puppies at the front door waiting for the mighty master to come home. We waited and waited to share our monumental accomplishment with Mom and Dad, competing for bragging rights as to whose efforts produced the winning result.

"I'm the one who got her walking," Sherl asserted, spirits high.

"You must be crazy! Don't you see those bruises and scratches on my knees from all that hard work?" I retorted, amid all the laughter, prompting Martin and Melony to take a glimpse at the bruises and scratches on their knees as well.

As the seconds turned to minutes and the minutes turned to hours, we continued to wait, late into the night. As we waited, we somehow fell asleep and later awakened to the bright sunshine of a new morning piercing through the sheets that we used for curtains over our windows. And still no Mom and Dad.

"I'm sure Mom and Dad will be home any minute, y'all know how they are," Melony said, playing down the desperation we were all starting to feel.

With no phone in our house, all we had was Melony's assurance that Mom and Dad would return to take us roller skating. Clinging to that small hope, we waited another day.

"Man, this is wrong! I hate the way Mom and Dad be doing us," I finally said by nightfall, no longer able to withstand my frustration.

"What did you say?" Melony asked in disbelief.

"I said I don't like the way Mom and Dad be doing us."

"You shut your mouth and don't you ever say nothing like that again!" Melony demanded putting an end to my frustrations. "You and Martin lie down, and I'll see you all in the morning," she concluded, tucking us in.

And so we spent another night hoping—hoping to see Mom and Dad, hoping to get our chance to go skating.

The following morning we woke to Melony bickering back and forth with what sounded like the police. I could hear the distinctive sound of their walkie-talkies cutting into the conversation.

"Young lady, we have called a social worker who will be arriving here any moment, and we need you and your brothers and sisters to go with her."

"Please don't take us. My mom and dad will be right back," she pleaded. "They just went to the store."

But the two sheriff's men knew something that we didn't know. Mom and Dad had been arrested for shoplifting and drugs and were headed back to prison again.

"I don't want to go!" I yelled. "I don't want to go!" Finally, the two sheriff's men picked me up and stuffed me into the backseat of the social worker's car where my sobbing siblings already sat, defeated.

Our ride to the crisis center was short, but I filled the car with much-warranted crying and screaming until I was hoarse and couldn't yell anymore. Seeing our few possessions being set out on the street moments before we had left hadn't helped, either.

This was the darkest night of my life. I lay sobbing my heart away in the foreign bunk bed of the crisis center, my face buried in a pillow soaked by salty tears and globs of snot from my runny nose. *Why! Why! Why do things have to be this way?* The time we spent in the crisis center still today is a void in my memory; but the nightmares of each night were the same daunting images that continued the breaking of my seven-year-old spirit.

# Chapter II

## *Trying To Face Another Day—Part 1*

"Kids, welcome to your new home. I hope you all in enjoy it here," were the last words we heard from our social worker, as she extended her arms to showcase the living room of our new foster parent, Ms. Mary.

And, with those words, I dropped my head in further defeat, opening up the floodgates of tears once again. *I can't believe this is happening!*

"Don't worry, Tommy, everything is going to be all right," Melony, Sherl, and Martin assured, fighting to hold back their own tears. "Everything is going to be all right." With Carmen now stripped from the four of us and in a different foster home, our future seemed to be very grim.

*Will I ever see Carmen again?* The thought of her being gone felt like a dagger through my heart. It was as if an infant had been snatched away from the bosom of her nurturing mother. And, with no answers to my lingering questions, my quest for stability went on.

Ms. Mary was an elderly, stern, short, full-figured woman from the Deep South who believed heavily in family. So much so, that she even refused to place her aging father in a nursing home, leaving the four of us to empty his urine- and waste-filled buckets each day. With Ms. Mary being so into family, her family members were around constantly, and we were expected to clean up after them, no matter whether it be a simple breakfast or a large family picnic.

"Y'all need to have this place cleaned up before y'all go to bed," she regularly demanded. "And if it ain't done right, y'all will be at it all night."

The two-story house in the middle of the block at 30th and Gaylord stayed spotless inside and out, thanks to us. At times, it seemed to me that the sole reason Ms. Mary had foster kids was to bring in free labor and a check from the state. Never did any of the money go toward new clothes. We were growing more and more accustomed to wearing hand-me-downs and second-hand attire from church clothing shelves and second-hand stores.

Wearing hand-me-downs and going to school with tough kids made my days long. There usually was not a day that went by when a classmate in the second-grade class of my new school didn't have something to say about the gear that I was wearing.

"Look at Tommy's shoes," the class jokester Tyrone shouted to the rest of the class the moment we all stepped a foot into the classroom. "Man, them shoes went out of style in the 1800s!" Of course, a roar of laughter swept throughout the classroom. Having no retort to minimize the grief from the other kids, I smiled on the outside and sobbed on the inside.

Adjusting to my new life at Ms. Mary's didn't come without a fight. The anger and hurt that I walked in with that very first day stayed with me for some time. It was destined to cause a lot of friction between us, just as it did with nearly everyone who came into my presence who was not my sibling.

My defiance toward Ms. Mary and her rules were not discreet. "I hate you, I don't want to be here, and I ain't doing nothing!" I would lash back at her when I'd had enough of being bossed around. Month after month this was my uproarious response toward her.

And it wasn't long before my resistance was met by whippings from her son Chuck.

"You see, Momma, what you got to do to this little nigga is break his spirit," Chuck would shout throughout the house while whipping me with whatever he could get his hands on. "I'm going to keep beating yo' ass around here, little nigga, until I'm tired." These whippings would clearly have been deemed abuse by state officials.

"You don't have to hit my brother like that," Melony shouted from across the room one evening after another one of these episodes. A shivering Martin and Sherl joined in her protest.

"Y'all better go in there and lay y'all's little asses back down before y'all get some of this too," he retorted, trying to catch his breath.

"We're not going anywhere until you stop hitting our brother." And, with those last words, the three of them joined me on the floor, and we all braced ourselves against the lashes of the extension cord that swung ferociously from the "want-to-be" dictator.

As the beatings continued and became worse and worse, each of us, on different occasions, ran away—out the back door, over the six-foot-high wooden fence in the backyard, and down the alley. My feet wouldn't stop until I rested safely on the front stairs of Aunt Milly's apartment.

"Please, please get us out of there, Auntie! I hate it there."

"Now, Tommy, I'm doing everything that I can ... but, in the meantime, you're going to have to go on back over there and do everything they tell you to do until I can help y'all," she stressed in a calm demeanor one day during our ride back to Ms. Mary's house. "Tommy, you have to try to listen to her."

With that in mind, I eventually began to keep my mouth shut and do what I was told, even when it meant playing the roll of host to the kids of Ms. Mary's visitors, something I rarely enjoyed doing.

One afternoon, a friend of Ms. Mary's came over with her son. "Kids y'all go on out in the front and talk to this nice young man," Ms. Mary said, sending us out into the front hallway.

The look on the tall, dorky boy's face told me that he probably didn't want to be there with us, just as much as we didn't want to be there with him. We boys sat in silence, not knowing where to start any conversation. The only entertainment came from the few whispers and giggling back and forth between Melony and Sherl. Their faces just seemed to glow with every glance at the boy. All of the giggling and whispering suggested to me that a crush on the boy was brewing. Meanwhile, the boy sat with Martin and me, looking puzzled by the behavior of the two girls. If they got a crush on this boy, they sho' ain't doing a good job of hiding it.

"Soooo, how old are you?" Melony finally asked, breaking the silence.

"I'm nine."

"Okay ... uhm what grade are you in?" Sherl added.

"Third grade," the boy sharply responded, which was one grade above me.

After more giggling and whispering, Melony presented another question to the frightened looking boy. "So, what is your name?"

"My name is Le." This response instantly drew excitement from both Melony and Sherl, who were now running and jumping throughout the hallway. "Yes! Yes!" they shouted, leaving the three of us dumbfounded as to the reason for the sudden joy.

And then suddenly came mind-blowing news from the two of them— news that I thought I would have never heard in my lifetime.

"Yes! Yes! Yes! You're our brother!" they shouted at the boy in unison with tears of joy.

"What! Our brother?" Martin and I couldn't believe what we'd just heard, and Le's dropped jaw exclaimed that he was just as stunned.

"What? Your brother?"

"Yes! Our brother!"

And, if there was any doubt at this point about Le being our brother, Melony and Sherl quickly cast them out by presenting the entire story to us about how he had been adopted by another family when we were all very young. His real name was Levi.

I was blown away by what I had just heard and witnessed. Our brother? And, like a river pouring into the ocean, we rushed to embrace each other, becoming one in our tears. For the first time in some time, I felt a sense of peace as I was able to hold a piece of me. This first-time introduction to my older brother brought joy into my hurting soul, and it had been a long time coming. The sobs from all of us showed that, even though we had been separated, we had somehow remained connected. I wanted this moment to last forever.

Then, suddenly, a distant voice yelled out, "Le! Le, put your coat and shoes on. It's time to go." And, so, our reunion came to an end.

As we watched him go out of the door with his adopted mother, my heart shattered into a thousand pieces. Our brief moment of sunshine had now turned into a thunderstorm of sorrow. That night I went to bed sobbing, not knowing if we would ever see Levi again.

*First Carmen and now Levi? Why? Why?*

And so life went on.

*Finally!* Our nearly one year of servitude at Ms. Mary's came to an end and we were all split up once again. Sherl moved out of state to Waterloo, Iowa, with her dad's side of the family, and Melony moved in with Grandma Mae. Martin, Carmen, and I moved in with Aunt Milly into her new three-bedroom apartment along with her three children on 24th and Downing. The move was bittersweet; we were reunited with Carmen, but we lost Melony and Sherl. It was confusing not knowing whether to shed tears of joy or tears of sorrow.

After some time with Aunt Milly, I overheard her one day on the phone explaining to someone that, during our stay with Ms. Mary, Carmen had been placed in the foster care of a white family, which was why her once-long, curly hair had now dwindled to only short broken strands. Her foster parents had probably not been informed by the social services that black hair requires moisturizers and gels to be healthy and look its best.

Being in a new place didn't halt my unruliness. Inside, I still felt unhappy, confused, and afraid. *How long will this arrangement last? Will living with Aunt Milly today lead to living with someone else tomorrow?*

Distrust, anger and destruction were becoming my best friends. I was mad at the world and adamant about unleashing havoc on others. When I was not getting into fights at school, I was getting into fights at home, usually with Donna and Martin.

"Tommy, you got to stop hitting on them like that," Aunt Milly constantly admonished me. *Whatever! They better leave me the hell alone.*

Outside the house, I was becoming the new neighborhood terror, and my special target was a kid named Jim. Jim never stood up for himself, making him fresh meat for me and the other bullies around the neighborhood. The fact that he lived only a couple doors down from us gave me easy access to him whenever I was not feeling good about myself, which was basically all the time.

Each day started with me throwing rocks at Jim and calling him names, which then led to a foot pursuit. "Wait until I get my hands on you, punk."

I'd chase Jim all the way home and up into his house, throwing punches at him and not leaving until I had shared a few choice words with his mom.

"Yo' ass is next, bitch," I would shout leaving her nearly speechless during my furious exit.

"Well, I never ..."

"Well, now you have. And I'll be back to kick Jim's ass again tomorrow," I'd yell, bursting out the screen door.

It was me against the world. I was a walking time bomb waiting to explode, full of self-destructive tendencies. I no longer dreamed about doing great things in the world and helping others; tomorrow in my eyes was only one more day of more pain, more sorrow, and less hope.

And when Jim was not around, I could usually be found throwing rocks at passing cars on the busy corner of 25th and Downing, yearning to see a multi-car pile up. Other times, I could be found destroying our local community gardens, not even once considering the many hours and months the senior citizens in our neighborhood had devoted to them. Each day, life was becoming less important.

As a third grader, I began to gain a strong interest in pocketknives, gangs, and sex. The most appealing of these three things was being in a gang. Gangs were just starting to sweep through the streets of Denver. The way the older teenage gang members hung out, protected each other, and were respected throughout the neighborhood was exactly what I was looking for. They were seldom challenged by anyone. That might, that power, was what I needed. And it would be just a matter of time before the opportunity would present itself.

That crossing of paths came about six months after my arrival to Aunt Milly's in the person of a flashy gangbanger named Crazy Boy, who weeks earlier had befriended Martin and I on the school playground. He became our potential avenue into the gang. Crazy Boy appeared to have it all—the shiny jewelry, the latest brand-name clothing and shoes, and, of course, he had the eyes and hearts of what seemed all of the teenage girls in our neighborhood. He had it all.

Our first tour of duty with Crazy Boy, in what we perceived to be the initiation process into the gang, brought us to one of the extravagant homes in a nearby neighborhood.

"Okay, this is what I want y'all to do. You see them bikes in that yard behind the garage? I want y'all to take all four of them, and then meet me behind the grocery store at the corner." We graciously accepted our invitation into the life of thievery; we passed with flying colors, taking all four bikes without being seen by any of the owners, who were sitting in the kitchen eating a family dinner.

Each day for weeks, we met Crazy Boy in the alley behind our two-story, brown-shingled apartment building, and our assignment was the same every day—stealing bikes of choice for Crazy Boy.

"All right. Y'all see them bikes sitting over there outside that corner store? I want y'all to take them and meet me behind that building across the street." And patted me on the back. "Don't look so scared, y'all are on y'all's way into the brotherhood," he said before scampering across the street to wait behind the mass of bushes at our assigned meeting point.

Hoping for a chance to be welcomed into the brotherhood of the gang, we headed off every day through alleys, over fences, and past vicious dogs to steal whatever Crazy Boy wanted. Day after day after day, this was our routine.

As the weeks continued to pass, it seemed we were no closer to being in the gang than we had been when we'd started the life of madness, not to mention the fact that we were now also giving Crazy Boy every piece of change we were able to find at home.

After stealing for days, I finally tried to stand up to Crazy Boy. "Man, we ain't with this stuff no more," I finally told him. "We are out of here," I concluded grabbing Martin's arm and heading home.

"Y'all are some little punks. So what y'all saying is, y'all don't want to be a part of the brotherhood!" Crazy Boy bellowed.

"That's right, we are done."

And that was the last day we ever saw the infamous Crazy Boy. Rumors later floated throughout the neighborhood that he got shot and killed in the midst of a home robbery.

But still, not even terminating my relationship with Crazy Boy could end my fascination with gangs. I became obsessed with the thought of starting up my own gang. We would be called the Captains, and I would be the head captain, of course. The idea of being the new ruler of our neighborhood burned like fire in me as I pondered how to bring the Captains into existence.

I daydreamed about seeing the name spray-painted on the walls of every building in my neighborhood. Also, I would have no problem challenging any punk who had a problem with me becoming the new ruler of our neighborhood. It was now my turn to become the one who had the latest fashions, jewelry, and all the ladies. The up-and-coming young boys in the neighborhood would have to seek me out for my approval for membership into the gang. I wanted to become "the man"—"the man" that everyone would respect and fear.

Fortunately, Aunt Milly had other plans for me. She sensed my urgency to be a part of something greater than myself. Her parental instincts told her that, unless something changed, I would end up either in jail or in a graveyard at an early age. I was headed for self-destruction.

Aunt Milly's plan involved getting me on the basketball team at a local recreation center, the Glenarm. As a third grader, I had never played basketball before, nor would I have been considered a kid with great athletic ability. But, through my involvement in basketball, I soon discovered that many of the same attributes that I yearned for from gangs were equally available through athletics. There was structure, brotherhood, rituals, camaraderie, and—best of all—we had a black head coach who provided us with a fun, secure, and stable environment. It was encouraging to me and my teammates to see a black man in this capacity … in a role beyond that of so many black men in our society. So many of us were used to seeing them jobless and the hopeless. And, of course, the girls liked athletes as well.

I wish that I could say that, after months of being involved in basketball, my academic performance and behavior improved in school, but it didn't. In fact, things were getting worse for me in school. Not only had I been placed in all the low-academic groups, I was starting to have more and more difficulty reading—especially when it came to reading aloud. I saw words backwards, misread words that looked similar to other words, and had difficulty in distinguishing small things such as the difference between "b" and "d", and "how" and "who." What's the problem? I know how to read! I had no idea at the time that I was suffering from dyslexia. The fact that I did not know this never gave me the outlet to use the words, "I have a learning disability," as a reason for not being able to read aloud. Mary Kay Ash, the founder of Mary Kay products, said it best when she said, "Aerodynamically the bumblebee shouldn't be able to fly, but the bumblebee doesn't know it, so it goes on flying anyway."

During my reading group, after hearing me read aloud, one student whispered to another, "Tommy's dumb. He can't even read!" How *humiliating*.

"Tommy, we just went over this lesson, and you're still not getting it," my teacher would often say rolling her eyes in great frustration, moving on to the next student.

In time, hearing these comments day in and day out, I started to question myself. *Am I really as dumb as many people think I am? Do I not get it?*

My doubting and questioning even began to impact the subject of math, which had always been a strong point for me. Only a year earlier, in third grade, I had put myself to the grueling task of learning all my multiplication facts through the twelves. Now in fourth grade, with everyone expecting me to fail, I failed. Failure became a self-fulfilling prophecy in my world.

Day after day, I retreated more and more into a shell of isolation and insecurity. Faced with the combination of struggling academically and being socially ridiculed, I kept the teacher from calling on me by initiating conflict in the classroom at the start of the day. And I discovered I could even get myself sent out of the room. *What a deal!*

"Tommy, stop it right now or I'm going to send you to the office," Ms. Border said, grabbing the supply of spitballs from my desk for the umpteenth time.

"I don't give a damn, send me to the office."

And to the office I went, to a place of no expectations, to a place of peace and solitude, to a place where I could sit at the lone desk in the back of the office.

Day in and day out, month after month, this was my strategy to keep the academic heat off. Deep down inside, a part of me yearned to be understood by Ms. Border or any other adult in the building. *Come into my world and talk to me, was what I* wanted most. My world was a place where many did not care or want to venture. It was a place that required endurance, patience, empathy, and understanding—skills that many educators simply did not have. And so I continued to fall further and further behind academically.

Unable to obtain either love or joy, I opted for the one other element that all human beings need in their lives—peace. My place of peace had become the Glenarm. Here I was invisible. Academics and family problems were not the standard by which one was judged. Here it was all about who had "game" on the court.

"Man, you can't hold me," was the phrase of confidence that came constantly from the mouths of the older players as I watched, mesmerized, from the bleachers.

"Oh, yeah? Well, show me yo' game. Show me what you got."

The gym was filled with oohs and aaahs from bystanders who were witnessing tricky plays and magical slam-dunks that would never reach the NBA, but were simply the product of the ambition to become "the man" in the land of street ball. No one ever ridiculed these players, despite the fact that many of them were high school dropouts. The Glenarm became my second home, keeping me engaged and feeding my appetite for connection and thrill.

The one thing I disliked most about living with Aunt Milly was making the dreadful trips to the local grocery store with what many of the kids at school referred to as "paper money." In our house, Aunt Milly simply referred to the paper money as food stamps. No matter what they were called, I hated every trip to the grocery store with them.

"Tommy, I forgot some things at the grocery store that I need you to go back and get." These words were sure to make me clench my fists, grit my teeth, and grumble under my breath from the moment the last words exited Aunt Milly's mouth. And it seemed it happened on a weekly basis. *Man! Why do I always have to be the one to go to the store with the food stamps?*

In my solo walk to Safeway Grocery Store or to Ace's Super Market, I always agonized over the long humiliating wait in line to buy food, and how all eyes seemed to zoom in on me when it came my turn to make my purchase and I had to fumble through the many pages of food stamp booklets.

*Man, I hate this,* I thought to myself as the store clerk loudly called out the number of stamps as I placed them in his possession. And if that was not bad enough, I then had to remove the food stamp booklet from my pocket to confirm that the serial numbers were legit with the numbers on the individual stamps.

Food stamps were familiar to many of the residents in the neighborhood, but it seemed that, in my moments of using them, I was always the sole recipient in the entire store. I stood in the shadow of cold stares of non-recipients who seemed to look down on those who received this type of government aid. As I stood in line, paranoid, all the jokes told at school about people who received welfare and got food stamps came to mind. One of the most popular was, "Your mama's so poor, she tried to buy tennis shoes with food stamps." It was a joke that always got a roar of laughter out of everyone in close proximity. Food stamps were issued only for the purchase of food items, hence the punch line for the joke.

Because of this stigma, I grew more and more petrified. Each time I stood in line, I tried to think of a new and creative approach to sliding the stamps from my pocket and into the hand of the cashier in the most discreet manner, hoping to avoid the gaze of surrounding onlookers. But it never seemed to work.

"You need one more stamp" or "You can't buy this with food stamps. It's not a food item." *How in the hell am I supposed to know that?*

It was as if, each time I got to the clerk, a big spotlight fell on my shoulders, showcasing me in my "moment of shame." Finally, one day I couldn't take it anymore. I had had enough. "Auntie, why you always sending me to the store with food stamps so everybody can look down on me and think that me and my family are poor and lazy?"

Her face looked baffled.

"Poor and lazy! Is that right? Well, Tommy, the truth is many people need a little pick-me-up from time to time in life, no matter whether it comes from family members or the government. You need to thank the Lord that you got some food to eat. Period. Don't you know there's people out there starving, wishing they could get food stamps? You need to see these here food stamps as a blessing."

After she said the words "starving" and "people" in the same sentence, she didn't have to say another word. I thought back to the many hungry, tearful, sleepless nights I had spent with my siblings in the past. Being seen as the heel of society wouldn't have mattered then if we could have gone to bed with our stomachs full instead of empty and growling. I left that conversation with Aunt Milly seeing her point clearly.

The true test of my emotions came during my stay with Aunt Milly, when Martin, Carmen, and I received notice from her that we were going to visit Mom at the Colorado State Penitentiary in Cañon City, a maximum security prison for women—whatever that meant. The thought of seeing Mom sent quivers of excitement through my belly. I couldn't wait!

"Fat Daddy," a close family friend, was in charge of taking us to see Mom. During our tiresome ride in his long, brown station wagon, I created picture after picture in my mind about how this place would look. *It has to have big, beautiful trees and parks, since it's so far away. And, oh yeah, it has to have lots of stores. Auntie Milly said there would be other women there, and women love shopping.* I continued staring out the window at the unfamiliar territory as we floated down the highway.

It had been over two years since we had last seen Mom, who had left without even a good-bye—and without taking us roller skating. In the pit of my stomach, a boiling war of emotions was raging. I longed to unleash all the pent-up anger and pain I had been harboring. *Why, why did you leave us? Why didn't we go skating? When are you coming back to get us?* Other emotions reminded me how sensitive Mom was and all that she had been through with Dad, and told me to just be happy and run and put my arms around her. But what I really felt like doing was crying—crying away all the sorrow. *But how can I cry when I'm filled with so much anger and pain?* I was learning to rarely give in to tears; they were a sure sign of weakness, and the last impression I wanted to give to Mom was that I was weak. I had to be tough; after all, I was her "big boy."

The prison was in a deserted area, surrounded by huge fences looming with rolls of razor-sharp barbed wire streaming across the top. Walking through all the gates with guardsmen possessing rifles was very intimidating.

"Open up gate one," the guardsman called into his shoulder radio, showing no emotion behind his dark sunglasses. The heavy locks unbolted and then closed again with a bone-jarring clanking behind us, re-securing the gate moments after we walked through. At each gate, we went through the same routine.

The sights and sounds of security cameras zooming above us, monitoring our every move, was just as frightening as the huge barbed wire fences and ferocious guards. Every corner inside the building seemed to hide a set of lurking eyes.

After being searched, we entered the waiting room where Mom would be joining us. No sooner did we sit down with other visiting guests, than the thick, lime-colored steel door opened at the far end of the room, and in came a group of women, all in brown shirts and brown pants, lined up single file and chained to one another. The line kept coming and coming until finally I saw Mom at the very end of the line. I debated whether to dash across the table and fall into her arms or run up and attack the guards for chaining Mom down like an animal. But all would be temporarily forgiven when I heard the soothing voice of Mom.

"Hello, sweethearts!" Mom said in the distance, fighting to hold back the tears as she picked up the pace toward our table. Her arrival at the table filled me with pure joy, and none of the emotions I'd felt earlier could outweigh my desire to embrace Mom and share tears of long-overdue excitement with Carmen and Martin. I felt like the prodigal son returning home after years of wandering in the darkness.

*Reunited*, yes! And it didn't take long to re-establish our connection. We spent what seemed like hours together laughing and joking, never once talking about any painful matters. *Man, it is great to be back in the presence of Mom again.* Dad, on the other hand, was a case of out of sight out of mind.

"Tom and Martin, y'all remember when I was going to make y'all smoke that whole pack of cigarettes to get y'all to stop picking up cigarette butts off the ground trying to act like ya'll were smoking when ya'll were younger? " Mom exclaimed, causing the two of us to cringe over the disgusting habit. "Y'all were some gross little boys."

We all laughed as I thought back to taking my first puff in kindergarten and nearly choking to death, ending my fascination with smoking.

"Yep, that was all it took," Martin replied. "We never picked up another cigarette butt after that day. At least I didn't," he concluded glancing at me with a look of sarcasm, implying that I may have dabbled with the butts a few more times before stopping.

I wanted this moment to last forever; however, saying good-bye was inevitable. The grins on our faces were brought to an end when the words, "Visiting hours are now over," rumbled from the overhead speakers. It was time to go. Mom, please don't go! I wanted to fight off the guards and demand that they not take Mom from me again. Paralyzed by a relentless flow of tears, I could do nothing. And, as before, I was further subdued with the pain of watching Mom being re-chained and handcuffed and escorted back through the heavy steel door.

I cringed at the awful sound of the closing door as it cut off Mom's last tearful glance at us.

The ride home was one of silent sobbing and many unanswered questions. My heart was broken, my soul fractured, my trust for the world minimal. The feelings of loneliness had resurfaced. *Will I ever see Mom again?*

# Chapter III

## *Trying To Stand Strong—Part 1*

Thunder Bird, Wild Irish Rose, and Night Train bottles had been left lying around. The carpet was old, balding, and bombarded with stains. The coloring of the walls was a hazed yellow, showing the effects of years of previous tenants who were probably smokers. Many of the pipes were fully visible, scaling the top of the ceiling or hovering close to the floor. There wasn't a new appliance in the place. The faucet in the kitchen constantly leaked, for not many hands in the house had the strength to fully turn off the water with the pliers that took the place of the knobs. Each chair around the small card table used for our kitchen table carried its own uniqueness—one a wood chair, one a silver folding chair, one a stool, and one a lawn chair. But this was her place, and she wouldn't have had it any other way.

"You know why they call this a shotgun house, Iron-pipe?" Grandma Mae often boasted, calling me by my nickname. "Reason being, if I were to take a shotgun and shoot it from that front door, the bullet would go straight through this house and out the back door without going through one single wall. It may be small and old, but its mine and it's all I got."

Mom and Dad assured us that these living arrangements would only be temporary. Carmen, Melony, Martin, and I were all now back in their custody. I was finally able to breathe a sigh of relief after not knowing over the past year if I would ever see Mom again.

Joining Martin and I in our new sleeping quarters in the living room was Grandma Mae's friend Claps, who was a very elderly man with limited mobility. His limited mobility made for long nights for Martin and me because he released his body waste into a huge Folgers coffee can that sat on the floor next to his couch during the middle of the night. Each night we were awakened and forced to plug our ears and noses in total disgust. The lingering smell was horrible, and many nights I wasn't sure if I could endure until the morning. Yuck!

The next "room," partitioned by a hanging sheet, would have been the dining room, but served as the bedroom for Grandma Mae and her boyfriend. And the "room" beyond that, partitioned by another sheet, was the nightly resting place for Mom, Dad, Carmen, and Melony. Climbing over and maneuvering around the maze of bodies on our way to the bathroom from "room" to "room" always called for extra caution at night. But, it was only going to be temporary, as Mom and Dad said.

As one could imagine, privacy in these conditions was pretty much impossible. Everyone's conversations just echoed from room to room. And, as time went on, I would discover a troubling truth about Mom and Dad.

It happened one night as I lay in bed. Grandma Mae was going into one of her drunken rages, which was the time Mom and Dad said she was most truthful. "I am so tired of them using my house for a shooting gallery for drugs. They steal all day long, sell all them damn clothes, but don't give me one damn dime. I can't believe that I let my drug addict daughter and her thieving boyfriend into my house," she shouted to her boyfriend in disgust.

*What? Mom and Dad, drug addicts and thieves?* I couldn't believe it. I struggled, hoping for a few more winks of sleep in preparation for school the following morning.

After days and days of pondering on Grandma Mae's words, it all made sense. All the times we had seen Mom and Dad come and go with the huge garbage bags of clothes. The times we had seen them go into the bathroom together and then come out after several minutes looking like zombies. Now it all made sense. The truth had been spoken. The feeling of betrayal simmered in my gut. *How could they do something like this?* I agonized with myself.

Living by the notion that a kid should always honor and respect his parents—ironically a phrase hammered home by Dad—I kept my mouth shut. Learning to never wince or cry aloud, I kept all my feelings bottled up, hoping that someday soon things would, in fact, get better.

After we had spent a little over a year on 26th and Curtis Street, a glimmer of hope came along when our family packed up and moved to the other side of town to *Park Hill. Wow! Park Hill!* It was exciting to be living in such a neighborhood as Park Hill, and a sure sign that things could be getting better. We moved to our rented duplex on the corner of 36th and Locust just before Christmas, my favorite time of the year. I was so elated.

Here at our new place I still did not have a bedroom, so to speak, but what I did have was seclusion in the wide space that I shared with Martin in the basement. The illumination of the room was poor, with sections of darkness scattered throughout the space because of weak lighting. Martin and I slept in the part of the basement that was partially carpeted with orange carpet, while Grandma Mae and her new boyfriend slept in the sole bedroom in the basement. Four windows ran across the top of each of the four walls in our space, two of which were covered by plastic that blew back and forth with the creeping nighttime breeze. The four surrounding walls were partially covered by dark wood panels that did little to insulate the space on cold winter nights.

This was the place that I called home in my new residence—a place where I could be found spending countless hours playing in the imaginary world of my toy soldiers. The chill of the room kept most outsiders away, which was exactly what I needed. The quietness, dim light, and cold provided perfect company and a safe haven for a teenager with a wounded soul and shattered self-esteem. It was difficult to survive by day on the outside of the space. But not here—here in this space I was invisible to the rest of the world.

Christmas Eve was almost upon us. Mom had just started working several weeks earlier, so things truly looked promising. I had spent most of my days leading up to Christmas Eve, when I was outside of the house, playfully quarrelling with my friend Larry about which of us was going to own bragging rights about the gifts we anticipated getting on Christmas day.

"Man, your little race track ain't got nothing on all the stuff I'm going to get in the morning," I said with confidence on Christmas Eve.

"Well, we'll just have to wait and see tomorrow then," he retorted, ending our conversation.

"Yeah, that's right, we'll see tomorrow."

All night I tossed and turned in anticipation of diving into the mountains of gifts that were going to be waiting for me upstairs in the living room the following morning. "Man, I can hardly wait!" I said to Martin, who was already fast asleep on the mattress and box spring identical to mine, resting on the floor.

After hours of tossing and turning, somehow I was finally able to fall asleep. I slept like a baby while visions of gifts danced in my head. A few hours later, I woke to the raspy morning voice of Martin, who was pulling at my covers. "Come on, come on, Tommy, let's go open up our presents. It's Christmas!" We dashed upstairs, where Carmen and Melony were already waiting in their pajamas.

After some discussion about who'd wake Mom and Dad to bring out the room full of presents, we forcefully bestowed the honor on Carmen.

"Go on, and hurry up. We ain't got all day."

The ruffling of bags in the room was like music to our ears. Mom followed Carmen back into the living room carrying a black plastic trash bag. Our eyes gleamed like stars as we waited to get our hands on our first set of gifts.

"All right, all right, y'all calm down now," Mom sternly said, while digging through the bag to pull out the first round of gifts.

"Okay, now that ya'll are quiet we can begin. Melony here's one for you—and you, and you, and you." She handed each of us a six-inch teddy bear from the bag.

Now a teddy bear was cool, but we were now ready for the real stuff. "Thanks, Mom!" Melony said.

"Yeah, thanks Mom!" Carmen, Martin, and I followed in unison behind Melony, battling each other to be first in line for the next gift.

The second gift out of the bag was a box of dominos for each of us, which we graciously accepted. By now the bag was completely empty, and we were ready to lead Mom back to the room to get the next bag of toys. After a little more battling for position for the next batch of items, we calmly stood in attention waiting for Mom to proceed back to the bedroom for more stuff.

And then, with a face of stone, Mom said, "That's it. That's all I have for y'all." She fell to the floor in tears.

*What! That's it? What do you mean by 'that's all'?*

We were in total shock, not knowing whether to be angry with her in the midst of this mind-blowing moment, or to comfort her. Still hoping somehow that it was a joke, we jumped to the floor to comfort Mom. *But there must be more. Come on, Mom, you have to be kidding, right? You must have overlooked the other gifts in the room,* I thought to myself, rubbing her back. "It's okay," I said.

On the inside of me it wasn't okay as I looked at the empty plastic bag lying crumpled on the floor. I was saddened and disappointed. She hadn't overlooked bags of gifts in the other room. That really was it. *So much for Christmas.*

We would later discover that old habits die hard. Mom had not been working anymore as Christmas Day approached, and she and Dad had gone back to their not-so-distant habits of stealing and doing drugs. Christmas Day for me would never be the same, and, in the days and weeks that followed, I would do everything in my power to avoid Larry, never speaking a word about Christmas to him or anyone else. And so life went on.

Each year, students in Colorado were given the grueling task of taking the Iowa Tests of Basic Skills to verify what they had learned and retained during the course of the school year. The guidance counselor visited my new seventh-grade class looked at me in complete disgust as he glanced over the horrific scores from my previous year of school. "I can't believe this …," he mumbled, walking away from me.

I remembered literally not even opening up the booklet to read the questions on the test that previous year, nonchalantly convincing myself that I had mapped out and broken the answer key for the test. Each question prompted a strategic answer of A, B, C, D, or All of the above. So much for that strategy.

My new school, Place Middle School, reminded me a lot of the prison where I had visited Mom when I was younger. There were high, towering fences surrounding the building, and dark, murky hallways. The only thing missing were the armed guards, whose presence might even have been helpful.

The older kids seemed to be a lot meaner than the elementary crowd. Over recess, most of us younger students clung to the doors waiting for the lunch bells to signal us inside. We warily watched the older students as they floated through the schoolyard pounding on anyone not in the eighth grade. I became the main target for many of the older boys since I was bigger than most of my seventh-grade comrades.

It didn't take long before skipping school became my new thing to do, in my effort to avoid both getting picked on and further academic ridicule. I was becoming a loner, spending more and more time wandering around off premises during the day until it was time to catch the school bus back to Park Hill from South Denver. I spent my days hanging out in parks and tossing rocks into the stream that ran a few blocks from the school, wondering, *Will I ever make it to age eighteen? What will I be doing when I get there?*

My grades were dropping faster than the stock market during the Great Depression. On the days when I did report to school, the looks and grades that I got from teachers strongly suggested that my academic future was going to be quite bleak.

"Tommy, if you don't start coming to school and doing better, we're going to have to notify your parents." I received this lecture over and over from teachers and administrators.

"I don't give a damn," I often snapped back, with a piece of me hoping that just maybe someone would call Mom and Dad. Maybe that would be a way for me to get some of their time and attention. "You can call whoever in the hell you want to call. It doesn't matter."

Despite my academic shortcomings, I was still able to somehow convince myself that maybe—just maybe—school may be important. So it would behoove me to try to at least attend on occasions. On one particular day that

I decided to show up, I became the recipient of a booklet that was distributed to our entire class. *Damn, the day I show up, it would be for a test!*

After closer examination of the cover of the test, I realized it didn't appear to be a typical one, judging by the creative graphics on the cover. With the test already sitting in front of me, it was too late for me to break camp and leave the room, and even too late to come up with an excuse to not take the test. I was stuck.

It had been some time since I had last been in class, and I was somewhat curious to find out what the test was about. With great hesitation, I opened the booklet. Minutes of thumbing through the pages brought me to the conclusion that, indeed, the test was different—it seemed to focus on creative ideas and problem solving, things I was quite familiar with. *Wow, this test looks fun! Working on someone else's problems for a while might be nice.*

Page after page, the questions seduced me into continuing. After a while, I glanced up at the clock. Man, it's been an hour! For the first time in a long time, I had finished a test—thoroughly and on time—with the rest of my classmates. Walking out of Ms. Johnson's classroom, I felt a sense of accomplishment for my engagement in what seemed to be a small and senseless test.

Weeks later, as I stood rummaging through my locker, I felt a hand came down on my shoulder. "Congratulations, Tommy," a deep voice behind me said.

"Congratulations? For what?" I turned around to see who this deranged person was. To my surprise, it was Mr. Edwards, our school counselor.

"Come with me to my office and I'll explain," he said, parting the jam-packed hallway of students who were preparing to whiz off to their next classes.

*Explain? Explain what? Maybe the school is getting ready to kick me out, and Mr. Edwards' words of congratulations are therapy for him because I'll be one less thorn in his side,* I thought to myself during the dreadful walk around the corner to his office.

"Come right in and have a seat while I get your file." After minutes of thumbing through the overfilled file cabinet of manila folders, he produced it—the infamous folder of Tommy Watson, full of nothing but copies of tardy and un-excused absence slips.

"Well, Tommy, you did a great job on the test you took in Ms. Johnson's class." He glanced at me with a look of surprise, and I returned the same raised-eyebrow look to him, for I had no idea what test he was talking about.

"In fact, you did so well, you will be placed in Mr. Evans' gifted and talented class, starting Monday."

*Gifted and Talented? I've never heard of any class like that.* I took the slip he handed me that stated the time and location of Mr. Evans' class.

"Good luck," he said, escorting me out the door.

I was completely puzzled the entire weekend, wondering if this gifted and talented class had something to do with athletics, since gym was a class I tried to participate in regularly.

I arrived on Monday morning to Mr. Evans' class—not just on time but, in fact, early. I took a seat in the very back of the room hoping to find out what this was all about. As the class filled up with other students, I began to peg their faces. These were not athletes; these were the academically astute. *These are all the smart kids! I got to be in the wrong place.* And from the looks that I was getting from several of them, I could tell they sensed the same thing. No sooner had I gotten up to slip out of the room, than the words "Tommy Watson" rang out.

"Tommy Watson … is there a Tommy Watson here?" The teacher looked up from his attendance sheet.

"Um, yes … yes, I'm here," I said, uncomfortably resting myself back into my seat. Wow! I am supposed to be here?

I couldn't believe it. I had actually qualified for this elite class based on my own merit. My heart pounded in excitement the rest of the day; I couldn't wait to get home to share the good news with Mom and Dad. For the first time in some time my self-esteem rose a notch, and I felt a sense of accomplishment.

I scrambled down off the school bus and ran the long block home after school. Bursting through the front door, I ran from person to person, sharing my good news and trying to articulate how much fun it was going to be being in the gifted and talented program.

"And I'm going to get a chance to go on field trips, and I'm going to get a chance to hang out with the smart kids, and …" After a few minutes of this enthusiastic behavior, I began to notice that no one in my family seemed at all interested in hearing my good news, including Mom and Dad. Disappointment washed over me. With a crushed heart, I quietly walked out of the living room and down the stairs to the basement, where I could lament alone. My accomplishment now seemed nothing more than trivial.

In the weeks that followed, I tried to do everything I could to stay involved and focused in the gifted and talented program, but self-doubt and the lack of family support cut into my ability to accomplish. They were the two things that separated me from all the other students in the program, and, without those two essentials, I was doomed. Eventually, I was kicked out of the program as a result of my lack of participation. I simply checked it off as another one of my life-long failures.

It wasn't long before we had to move again. With that move, we found ourselves back in Five Points, living at the corner of 23rd and Humboldt in a huge gray house that highly resembled Castle Greyskull where He-Man hid out in the Masters of the Universe comic. I would spend the remainder of my seventh-grade year at a new school, Morey Middle School, with many of my old friends.

And once again everything from the past resurfaced in our house, including the fights, the drugs, the alcohol, and the stealing, I turned back to the same place that I had missed during my time away—the Glenarm—as a place of peace. Basketball kept my mind off the problems at home.

"All right, fellas, here's the deal. No grades, no basketball. If you don't maintain a C average on your report card, consider yourself off this team," was the demand of our basketball instructor, Coach Maxey.

This was going to be a tough demand on me, given the fact that my previous semester's report card from Place Middle School had been full of Ds and Fs. If the Glenarm and basketball were to remain a place of peace for me, I would have to meet the challenge and get my grades to at least a C average and maintain that level, which, surprisingly, I did through the remainder of the school year.

Morey Middle School was the home school to many of the kids from Five Points and from the projects that bordered Five Points and downtown. It was a school that had a reputation for being one of meanest and roughest middle schools in the city. Broken homes and repeated generations of poverty seemed to be the commonalities many of us shared. And it was a sink-or-swim environment at school. Either you found yourself being part of the problem, or you found yourself being victimized by the problem makers. When I saw the physical and psychological damage done by the problematic students towards their victims, it didn't take long for me to elect to dive into the action and become a part of the problem.

When we were not throwing rocks and damaging school buses from other schools during the week days, my Morey comrades and I could be found at Celebrities Fun Center wreaking havoc on students from rival middle schools. Every weekend, battle began with a sneak attack, as we crept through the back and side doors with sticks, rocks, and bottles. And ... Bam! By the end of the battle at least one student from our rival schools would be knocked out cold on the floor, while others ran and stumbled from Celebrities with bleeding heads and faces. The excitement and the opportunity to brag in school on Monday mornings kept us coming back every weekend.

"Man, can't nobody touch our school. And if they try, they going down," Big Elwood yelled throughout the cafeteria. He was a student who was all too familiar with the battles, given the fact that he had spent his last two years in the same grade participating in them. "That's right!" The rest of us concurred.

For months and months, the fights continued at Celebrities, becoming more and more vicious each time. Now many of the battles were concluded with mobs of police speeding through the streets of the small area of Glendale that was home to Celebrities, in search for us as we scrambled back onto the city bus headed back to Five Points. Ambulances also filled the parking lot tending to the victims. Finally, by the beginning of the summer, management put a halt to the problems by banning middle schoolers from the premises.

The only other place left for us to hang out for the summer was a local nightclub near the projects called Breezin. It was a hole-in-the-wall teenage club. Here, one never had to show any ID. You just paid your $4 entry fee and had a good time. Nearly every dime of my Summer Youth Employment check was spent on Breezin, and on outfits to wear.

Every weekend, I'd get dressed up and head on down to the club with a couple of my comrades from school and the basketball team, Charles and Michael. It was always the same routine—they came to get me, we would drop in to the local Safeway grocery store, run to aisle seven, slap on half a bottle of Brute cologne, and then proceed to make the mile-long walk together, laughing and joking.

One day, we were in motion through one of the school yards, just three blocks from the club, when, suddenly, Charles pulled a joint from his pocket. I was shocked and couldn't believe it. *A seventh-grader with marijuana?*

"Man, what the hell is that?"

"It's weed, stupid. Haven't you ever seen weed before?"

"Well, uh … what you doing with some weed?"

"Michael, tell this fool what we about to do with this weed," said the mischievous Charles.

"We's about to get blown away," Michael retorted, taking a puff with his head cocked back as if he were getting ready to ascend into the heavens.

After passing the joint back and forth between the two of them for a minute, Charles reached over to me with it and said, "It's your turn."

I stood motionless, not knowing what to do. Meanwhile, Michael was running around in the middle of the street, laughing and coughing and choking—obviously feeling the effects of being high.

"So, what you going to do?" Charles said, reaching to put the joint in my hand. "Don't be no wuss, man." I had a dilemma on my hands. *What should I do? If I don't smoke it, they're probably not going to think I'm cool anymore. On the other hand, if I do smoke it, I might become a drug addict.*

Back and forth I went battling with myself, when suddenly the images ran through my mind of the effects that drugs and alcohol had had on Mom, Dad, and Grandma Mae. And that image right there was enough to seal my decision.

"Nah, man."

"Man, take the stuff," Charles insisted.

"Nah, man, I don't mess around with that stuff. I'll leave that to y'all."

And that was the end of all conversation about it, and they never offered me marijuana again. And, to my surprise later on, they both seemed to respect me for my decision. More importantly, I was proud of myself. And, at that very moment, I made a pledge to myself that, of all the things in the world I might do, drugs and alcohol would not even be on the list of options. To this day, I am proud to say that I have stayed true to my pledge.

Later on that summer, Breezin had become one of the most violent clubs in the city of Denver. The territory of Breezin and its surroundings was now being claimed and occupied by one of Colorado's most notorious gangs. The gang included local members as well as many members who had migrated from Compton, Watts, Inglewood, and other communities in California. The days of hand-to-hand combat and fighting with sticks and rocks were over; the many victims of the new violence were introduced to the power of shotguns, semi-automatic weapons, and group stomp downs, not to mention violent kicks in the face, head, stomach, ribs and any other vital areas by groups of ten and sometimes twenty gang members until unconsciousness set in—or death. Man, these guys are brutal!

Residents in the neighborhood of Five Points now began making daily checks of their wardrobes, making sure the colors of their clothes were in compliance with colors demanded by the new "sheriffs" in town. If you didn't wake up each morning and go over your daily wardrobe to make sure it met the dress code, you were in danger, and the possibilities were bodily harm or death. It soon became understood for many of the residents in Five Points, both young and old, that there was one color in particular that had to be eliminated from our attire. The color red was forbidden. No más! But still there were those who didn't know about the dress code, or decided they were not going to abide by this new way of life. In either case, it didn't take long before they were confronted, jumped, beaten, and, in some cases, even killed for wearing red. Knowing the consequences that rested before us, many chose to find other favorite colors. Myself, I got rid of red and adopted blue.

Meanwhile, things at home showed no signs of changing, and it wasn't long before the madness in our house started to spill out into the streets, revealing to our neighbors that our household was definitely not a normal home.

One afternoon, as Melony and I were sitting downstairs watching my favorite show, *Sanford and Son,* we heard banging and hollering from Mom and Dad's room upstairs. Both of them had just come home moments earlier and had headed upstairs for their normal routine of shooting up drugs in their room.

Within seconds, Dad came running down the stairs, screaming, hollering, and jumping everywhere. "Get 'em off of me, get 'em off of me!" he shouted.

Melony and I looked at each other, wondering what the heck he was talking about. Other than the fact that his brown bell-bottom pants clashed with his blue butterfly-collared shirt, everything seemed fine with him.

"Dad, what are you talking about?" I yelled, trying to get him down from the couch.

"Don't you see 'em? Snakes! They all over me!" He streaked off the couch and bolted out the front door, screaming into the crowds of neighbors who were enjoying the beautiful summer afternoon.

By the time Melony and I put our shoes on and got to the front door, he was already running down the middle of the street, continuing his escapades and screaming about the snakes that were crawling all over him. Cars veered, blowing their horns, to keep from hitting him, and onlookers fled out of his path. Soon, nearly all our neighbors were on their front porches, trying to figure out where all the commotion was coming from. As Melony and I ran past the crowds of onlookers in pursuit of Dad, who was now trying to climb the stop sign at the corner a block away, whispers of "He's crazy!" and "That man is a damn fool" floated through the air.

Every time we nearly caught up with Dad, he showed us why he had been a high school track star, leaving us in the dust as he scampered over the tops of parked cars and over fences. After several blocks, we were finally able to corner him in the backyard of one of the local residents, who was gazing disapprovingly out her window at his antics.

"It's okay, ma'am, we got him," the two of us said, hunched over and out of breath.

"Well, you get that crazy man out of here before I call the police on y'all."

"We will," we exclaimed grabbing Dad by the arm.

We made the journey back to the house with Dad between us, clinging to our arms. It seemed like everyone in the neighborhood was outside by now, whispering to each other and laughing about what had just taken place. The looks on their faces led me to believe they suspected this was a classic case of Dad using some bad drugs—otherwise known as "getting wooed." He was lucky; many individuals who had a reaction like that ended up in the hospital or the graveyard. Facing my friends after this incident was tough, but I somehow managed.

The end of the summer brought even more hardship. Out of the clear blue one day, the local sheriffs greeted us at our front door.

"Good day, folks, is this the Watson residence?"

"Yes it is," Melony, Martin, and I curiously responded.

"Well, we have been instructed by the owner of this house and the courts to remove you all from the house and off the premises at this time," they intoned. *What? Remove us from the premises? But this was supposed to be our new home.* "Please step aside."

And with those words from the sheriff's men, the assault on our possessions began, as they sent us, along with our possessions, crashing out into the front yard. I couldn't believe it.

With Mom and Dad nowhere around, as usual, we scrambled through the front yard trying to salvage what we could. *I can't believe this is happening!*

By the time we were finally forced from the house, our watchful neighbors had learned more about our chaotic household. Some of them stood in shock, holding their mouths, while others turned their heads and snickered, trying to avoid eye contact with us.

On the outside I looked numb to the sad and painful reality of what was taking place. "Everything is all right, it's just a misunderstanding," I said trying to make a defense to several of my schoolmates. Deep inside of myself, however, I wanted to fall to the ground and cry, but too many of my days had been spent that way, and, no matter how badly I wanted to give in to that temptation, I was not going to do it—especially not in the public eye.

Eventually, we could only stand speechless in front of neighbors and friends who continually asked, "Why y'all getting thrown out?" The sheriff's men continued for what seemed like hours clearing out the house from top to bottom. So many things were being thrown from the house that we couldn't retrieve and gather them quickly enough. *How humiliating this is?* With every piece of clothing, every piece of furniture, and every item of food from the five-bedroom house lying before me in the yard that was about the quarter of the size of a football field, the battle not to cry in defeat ate at me like a can of hungry maggots.

Finally, by dusk, a friendly voice spoke from the chatty crowd that was starting to assemble around the yard.

One elderly neighbor approached us and directed his head to the vultures waiting for the first sign of darkness when they could take whatever possessions they could from the front yard. "Hey, I'll tell y'all what, y'all can put some of the stuff that you really need in my garage, because y'all know once night falls you won't see it again." We moved with great haste, trying to put clothes for each of us into the garage, knowing we were only minutes away from a lurking night sky.

As night did finally come upon us, the elderly man's words of prophecy came into fruition. Dozens of voices cried out from the pitch-black yard we use to call home. "Man, I'm taking this right here," and "Come on, hurry up and grab that over there." So we walked away, helpless to fend off the scavengers, looking for the nearest payphone so we could try to track down Mom and Dad.

*Man, I can't believe this. God really must have something against me and my family.* I looked around at our new home, the Triple A Motel—cigarette-burned carpet, one window, two beds, and a bathroom, $35 per night—resting on the outskirts of Denver in a place called Commerce City. One lousy motel room to house nine miserable lives. It would be the first of two different motel rooms that we would call home over the next year and throughout the course of my eighth-grade year of school. Disheartened, at best, described my state of mind.

Nine of us occupied the small confines of the room: Melony and her boyfriend Phillip, who had just gotten kicked out of his mom's house earlier that summer after he and Melony were caught smoking crack cocaine; Grandma Mae and her boyfriend, who were continuing their drinking frenzy all day, every day; Mom and Dad, who were still heavy heroin users and into shoplifting; and, finally, of course, there were Carmen, Martin and I, the only sober individuals in the place. Nine dark futures behind a door sign that urged "Do Not Disturb."

Bundles of sheets held our clothes. Piles of shoes were stacked beside the small refrigerator that was tucked into the corner near the television. A two-burner hotplate cooked most of our meals that didn't come from Church's Chicken.

When we were not eating Church's Chicken, we were introduced to one of Grandma Mae's "exotic" meals that looked and tasted like mush soup. Green beans, corn, okra, potatoes, peas, and anything else she could throw into the small simmering pot became dinner.

The stench in the room was an awful, musty combination of cigarette smoke and mildew. The poor lighting gave the room a cave-like effect, which was further enhanced by Mom and Dad's paranoia for open curtains. The cockroaches traveled at will and always found some hidden space in our clothing. They revealed themselves at the most inappropriate times—like falling from my shirt onto my desk in the middle of the school day, causing fright and laughter among my classmates. Why? Why does life have to be like this?

Feelings of betrayal and resentment toward Mom and Dad surfaced in me, especially toward Dad. He was the loud voice from the past, always raving about how he was the man of the house. I began to hate the so-called "man of the house." "What's wrong with you now?" Dad asked, hands on his hips and sucking his teeth, after finding me crying on the bed one evening.

"I'm tired of living like this. Why can't we be like normal families?" I said, still sobbing.

"What! A normal family? What the hell you know about a normal family, you ungrateful little bastard? We are a normal family," he said in a brutal tone, "And, if you don't like it, you can get the hell out of here," he concluded storming into the bathroom, leaving me in more tears and with a stronger feeling of hatred toward him.

In school, the constant heckling that I got from others never seemed to cease. Many of the students held daily joking sessions in the classroom and lunchroom—and I was the object of their jokes. Most of the laughter centered around our family car, or "the hearse," as many of the Morey students referred to it. Our car was an older model 1970s station wagon whose trip to the junkyard was long overdue. The two darkly colored, spray painted doors clashed with the lighter brown body. The large, broken rear window had been replaced with a huge piece of plastic. Only one headlight strained to provide nighttime vision. The antenna was large and limp, the tip almost resting on the hood of the car. The muffler was filled with holes. With every backfire, heads turned and hearts pounded from the sound. Whenever Dad flipped on the turn signal, the radio would instantly shut off until the signal went off. Needless to say, the wagon was in pretty bad shape.

Each morning when we pulled up to the schoolyard to be dropped off, the place suddenly came alive. Hecklers throughout the playground yelled out to submit their best "put down" about the wagon.

"Hey, ain't y'all late for the funeral down the street?" someone would shout, igniting rumbles of laughter throughout the jam-packed schoolyard.

"They're going to be having your ugly mama's funeral soon, if you don't shut the hell up," I'd shout back to the crowd, who continued laughing, paying me no mind.

Even the brakes gave us trouble. "Oh, no! Oh no, there they go again," Dad often complained on our way to school, pumping the brakes and turning the steering wheel to avoid the cars waiting at the red light in front of us. He finally resorted to the art of using the emergency break to bring us to a complete stop each day. Seeing Dad in this panic always gave us a laugh and eased some of the tension and silence in the car. The thought of a possible accident due to brake failure never even crossed our minds as Dad sat in the driver's seat wiping the sweat from his eyebrows after stopping within inches of the car in front of us.

In gym class, my teacher Mr. Wilburn continued the attacks. Immediately following roll call each morning, he would cut loose on me. "Hey, did anyone see Tommy's Grandma pushing their car up to the school this morning?" The gym, of course, would fill with laughter.

"I didn't see that, but I did see the funeral home cops escorting them into the school parking lot," someone else said, keeping the laughter going. Ha-ha-ha.

Each day the jokes came from every direction and were too many for me to fend off. My skin on the outside appeared thick, but, on the inside, I was embarrassed and hurt. To admit to the pain would only bring more ridicule. Being a person who couldn't stand the heat of jokes or "ranking," as we called it, only gave the rankers more ammunition for their assault. Weathering these storms had to be done in silence.

Finally, one morning I had a brainstorm. "Mom, can we get out here so we can get some candy before school?" I asked one morning, motioning towards the 7-Eleven around the corner from our school.

"Sure, but ya'll better go straight to school afterwards."

Martin and I got out of the car and went into the store. We hid behind the racks of candy for which we had no money. We waited for Mom and Dad to drive off, and then walked right back out of the store and on to school.

The plan was marvelous, and I even boasted to Martin about how brilliant I was. "Man, if we ever have a little brother, you better show him the ropes to life like I be showing you. You don't know how lucky you are to have a big brother as smart as me."

Day after day, week after week, all was well with the masterful plan. In the door of 7-Eleven we went—and out the door we came as soon as Mom and Dad drove off. It was magnificent, and temporarily eased some of the school slander. But it didn't last forever.

All was well until, one day, Mom caught wind of our little game to get to school without ridicule. I was never quite sure how she exposed my extraordinary plan. In no time, we discovered just how good we'd had it before we tried to pull one over on her.

"Y'all think y'all's slick? Well, I'm going to show y'all," Mom said with a stern look. And the days of pulling up in front of the school and letting us out of the car to a couple of giggles were over.

Each day, Mom and Dad put on quite a show as they dropped us off right in the dead center of the school bus lane, which sat directly in front of the school. "Hey everyone, here's Tom and Martin," Mom would shout, reaching over to continuously blow the horn while Dad sat chuckling under his breath and leaning back in the driver's seat to give Mom free access to the horn. "That's right everybody, here they are, tell them good morning," she'd again shout, as the two of us bolted from the car and into the school amid storms of laughter.

As if the school yard humiliation wasn't bad enough, Mom took things a step further. Each time we saw pretty girls, traditionally Martin and I would duck to the floor so we couldn't be seen in our notorious station wagon. Instead of just driving past the girls now, Mom would blow the horn, getting their attention. Then she'd pull up next to them and ask in her sweetest voice, "Do y'all know Tom and Martin?" Of course, the girls' response was a big, fat "No!"

"Well, I want y'all to come over here and meet them. They're in the back, hunched down on the floor." She'd motion for them to come take a peek through the back window while she poked her fingers into the tops of our ducked heads, explaining who was who and how old we were. "That's right, this one right here is Martin, and he's thirteen, and that one over there with the coat over his head is Tom, and he's fourteen."

"Yep, I have the smartest big brother in the world. Thanks, big brother," Martin often added in disgust.

After going through this day after day, week after week, it didn't take long for us to realize that the game Mom was playing with us had an underlying message, which was to be thankful, and take pride in whatever we had. Our lesson in the school of thankfulness had to be learned the hard way, but we learned.

Despite the few fun moments we had together, life at home was still chaotic, and so, to keep my inner peace, I continued to turn to playing basketball for the Glenarm team. No one at school or at the Glenarm knew of my living arrangements in a motel, and, because the school had only Aunt Milly's address as my home address, no one would ever know.

Each day after school, I grabbed a quick bite at Aunt Milly's and went immediately to the Glenarm to work on my game. I also spent hours outside of practice working on my jumpers, free throws, layups, and defense. And that year I eventually developed into one of the better players on the team, which gave me an opportunity to better maintain my sanity. Having a sweet game on the court always alleviated some of the pressures I felt in the world outside of sports. And having the reputation as an athlete was vitally important, because the only other alternative that got as much attention—and probably more respect in the land of Five Points—was being a gang member. My teammates and I all vowed to never take part in gangs.

By now, many people throughout the city of Denver had begun referring to Five Points as "Little Compton." This was because of the large numbers of gang bangers who had come into the city from Compton, California.

"Man, gangs can only take you to one of two places—to the graveyard or to the penitentiary," said our team captain Tyrone one day, getting nods of "Amen!" from the rest of us. "Man, them fools are out there killing each other for no reason."

And, despite the pledge of good faith we had all taken, the vast majority of my teammates would later go on to get sucked into the gang lifestyle, costing many of them their freedom and, in several instances, their lives.

As the basketball season progressed, the team was surprised one afternoon following one of our games by a group of high school coaches from a suburban, predominately-white, private school called Mullen—a school that sat minutes away from the site of the most deadly school shooting in America, Columbine High School.

"All right, fellas, let me have your attention. I have some gentlemen here today who want to talk with you all about an opportunity that could do many of you a lot of good," Coach Maxey said, turning things over to the coaches from Mullen.

"Thank you, Coach Maxey. We're here because we think you all are a very fine group of athletes, and, from what we hear from your basketball coach, a very fine group of students in the classroom as well. We want to extend an invitation, to those of you who would be interested, to become students at Mullen High School next year—provided you take and do well on the entrance exam, which is coming up in a few weeks. We'd love to have you come to our school and take part in our sports program. Many of the young men who come to our school to play sports and stay focused on the academics do well and go off to college on athletic scholarships," the gentleman concluded. "I will let your coach know about the dates for the test. Thank you."

Yes! My teammates and I were ecstatic about the possibility of attending such a prestigious high school, which was well known for its sports program and for sending athletes to college.

"Man, I'm about to go home and tell my mom about this right now," our starting point guard Little Earl shouted with joy. "Me too" echoed around the gym from the rest of us. Up to this point, not many of us had ever thought about the possibility of going to college. Our eyes had been focused only on the NBA; we were not sure how or why going to college would fit into the equation. Excited as I was, I knew deep down inside that I was probably the player on the team who was least likely to pull off the daunting task of convincing Mom and Dad to see how I could benefit from going to such a school. *How am I going to tell Mom and Dad about this?*

During my long walk back to the motel room, I also thought about the unfortunate and agonizing experience with Dad just months earlier, when he accused me of being selfish, and about the lack of support I was given in my involvement with everything else. *They probably won't take it too well that I'm ready to try something different, in a school where they may have to pay some money.* So I decided to wait and see if I could raise my academic performance to a B average and work on my attitude in school—both of which were necessary elements for acceptance into Mullen.

In the months that followed, I was nominated by the first teacher to ever see signs of potential in me, Mr. Tabono, for the Colorado Youth Citizenship Award, which I would later go on to win. I became the One-on-One Basketball Champion of my eighth-grade class (with Martin doing the same for the entire seventh grade). I also became the Heavyweight Wrestling Champion after "accidentally" breaking the nose of my opponent, who weighed nearly a hundred pounds more than I. The honor roll, which before had sounded to me like nothing more than a catchy movie title, included my name throughout the remainder of my eighth-grade year. I even volunteered my time to coach some of the younger kids playing sports in the neighborhood, one of whom would go on to become an NBA star by the name of Chauncey Billups.

By spring, I was rolling with confidence, especially when I found out I had passed the entrance exam for Mullen, which I had discreetly taken without Mom or Dad's permission. With this part of my journey complete, it was time to break the good news to my parents.

I told them one morning as we were all preparing to leave our motel room and hurl through the struggle of a new day. "Guess what? I've been accepted into Mullen High School. I already passed the test, and the only thing left for me to do is pay the $200 registration fee." I explained the situation to Mom and Dad and tried to assure the two of them that their commitment would be minimal.

"What? Mullen. Ain't that that school where all them white folks go? Boy, get yo' butt in that car and sit down somewhere. You ain't going to school with all them white folks. They don't want you out there with them no damn way, and we sho' ain't about to be paying no money for you to be going to nobody's school," Dad snapped back, crushing all hope I had conjured up and sapping the energy right out of me.

For weeks I cried and moped around in disgust, showing very little of my face to the outside world. *Why do I have to have parents like this? Will I ever be able to make something of myself?*

A month later, the ending of the school year coincided with a phone call that dropped Grandma Mae to her knees in tears. "O, Lord, I don't know what we going to do now," she said, hanging up the brown phone that sat on the small table between the beds in our motel room. "What are we going to do?"

"What's wrong, Grandma?" We all sensed the urgency of the phone call.

"That was Betty, y'alls mamma's friend, and the news she told to me ain't good. She said that y'all's mama and daddy just been picked up by the police for shoplifting and they headed back to the joint." She started sobbing again.

I was stunned by the news. *What?* Disbelief swept over me, while fear of the unknown started my body shaking with the panicked thought of being separated once again from my family. In the days that followed, Betty's news was proven to be true—Mom and Dad were headed back to prison again. We were kicked out of our motel room, and the owner retained many of our possessions for rent not paid. Once again we were headed down the scary slope to darkness, not knowing what tomorrow would bring.

# Chapter IV

## *This Pain I'm Feeling—Part 1*

Grandma Louise was flabbergasted by the beauty of the campus. And I couldn't agree with her more as we stepped from the last of our three-bus, one-hour ride to the school from Five Points. Grandma Louise had opted to move out of the nice quiet retirement home to take in Martin, Carmen, and me after Mom and Dad's incarceration. Despite the fact that we now lived in the heart of the drugs, violence, and poverty of Five Points, knowing that I would now be attending Mullen High School offered a glimpse of hope for the future.

"Boy, I want you to come out here and do well, you hear me?"

"Yes, ma'am, Grandma. I'll try to do my best,"

We continued walking, mesmerized by the lovely array of flowers that edged the pathway leading past the pond in the middle of the campus.

"I want you to enjoy every last minute of this place," Grandma Louise concluded, looking around at the freshly cut, grass.

We were right on time for our 9:00 am meeting to discuss the finalities for my entry into the school with the varsity head football coach Pete Levine, who assisted those of us from underprivileged communities. At the time, I could never have imagined that stepping into his smoke-hazed office would be the beginning of a miraculous relationship with a man I would grow up to see as being part of my own family.

Coach Levine, who had grown up under pretty harsh conditions in his Jewish community on the East Coast, was a no-nonsense type of guy, much like Grandma Louise.

"Good morning. You come on right in and have a seat," Coach Levine yelled from across the desk that was flooded with football videotapes. "Did you have any problems finding the school?"

"No problems at all. The directions from the bus service were perfect," Grandma Louise said, taking her seat and cradling her infamous pocketbook in her lap.

With the conclusion of our greetings, it was time to get down to the business at hand. The first thing Grandma Louise wanted to know was, "Will my boy be able to come out here and graduate from this here school?"

Coach Levine's straightforward answer, as he extinguished the last of his cigar, was, "If Tommy comes here and works his butt off like everyone else, he will surely graduate."

With that hurdle out of the way, it was on to the next and most important question from Grandma Louise. "How do you reckon we will be able to pay all these thousands of dollars for his schooling here?"

"Well, one of things we offer here is a partial scholarship that will cover half the tuition for families who can't pay the full amount. The other half can be paid by the family, or the student can work hard on campus to cover the rest of the tuition."

Now, if there were any two words that a person could say to get Grandma Louise's attention, they were the words "work" and "hard"—words that didn't always sit too well with me. But it was too late now. Coach Levine was speaking her language.

"Hmmm, sounds interesting. Tell me more about this work 'thang,'" she said, leaning forward in her chair.

*Come on, Grandma, go on and pay this man the money so we can get on up out of here. A mellow sigh slipped from my lips as I purposely adjusted myself in the chair.*

"Do you need to use the toilet or something, boy?" Grandma Louise asked me in her most serious of faces, sensing my irritability. "Ah, ah, no, ma'am. I am fine." She turned back to face Coach Levine. "Sorry about that. Go ahead with what you was about to say."

"We provide students with the chance to work either in the cafeteria during the school year or outdoors here during the summer. He stretched out his arms to showcase the campus from his window.

There was no stopping her now. "Is that right? Well, good. What these kids need nowadays is some hard work. Tommy, he can start right now," she said, leaving my mouth to drop wide.

"What … right now?" I looked for a sign that this was just some bad humor from Grandma.

"Boy, don't you give me that look," she said, standing up and handing me the bus schedule and change from her pocketbook. "I'll see you when you get home."

Grandma Louise never looked back as she headed down the stairs and out to the bus stop. I couldn't believe it. She was dead serious about me beginning work right then and there.

Meanwhile, I was led to a patch of weeds beneath the football stadium bleachers to begin my orientation to the world of hard work. Needless to say, that day, the rest of that summer, and the summers that followed, I discovered first hand how Mullen stayed so beautiful and magnificent.

With the start of school came also the opportunity to get new clothes. The dress code at Mullen required slacks, dress shirts, and no tennis shoes. Operating with a limited income, Grandma Louise squeezed four pairs of pants and four shirts out of her budget, which I learned to rotate and wash each week, showing no signs to the outside world of any lack in my wardrobe. I cured my ignorance about tying a tie by studying a "learn to tie your tie" booklet—also from Grandma Louise.

Being one of only six blacks in my freshman class was definitely a twist from living in a predominately black neighborhood and attending predominately black schools. Later on during my tenure at Mullen, those numbers dropped even more sharply when Kevin, Terry, and Ralph, three young men from my neighborhood, were kicked out of the school for academic failure and social misconduct.

Social misconduct basically meant playing the fool and thinking that we were accepted by the white kids at the school, who spent countless hours talking about the three of them behind their backs. "Those guys are idiots," the white kids would whisper to each other in the lunchroom, as Kevin, Terry, and Ralph put on a public show for them, talking about each others' moms, jumping on tables, and running around the jam-packed cafeteria calling each other "nigga."

"Man, y'all need to chill out acting like fools just to befriend these white folks who are only talking about y'all behind y'all's back," my new best friend Bobby and I warned the three of them one day. Bobby was also the only one who knew about my family situation, the result of a slip of the tongue by me.

"Ah, man, y'all just jealous. Y'all don't know what y'all talking about. They like us." And they'd run off through the crowded hallways, hooting and hollering.

In the end, all three created their own fate. The white kids constantly talked about them and told on them for cheating and copying their homework. Ultimately, they landed back in the neighborhood and adopted the infamous words of many, "Man, the white man is the reason that I am who I am and why I do what I do today." I often saw them on corners selling drugs and drinking with the other neighborhood locals in Five Points. Someone once told me that, when you blame another man for your actions, you give him power and dominion over you, essentially saying that you can't survive or achieve anything unless you have the stamp of approval from the person you blame for your own faults. And each of these individuals seemed less and less empowered with every dripping excuse and complaint from their mouths as they sat on the corner letting their lives dwindle away because of incarceration and drug addictions.

Bobby, my man Des, and I shared a philosophy. We believed that we were at Mullen for no reason other than to play sports and to possibly make an attempt to graduate. And we pledged that we would take the next incoming class of black students from our neighborhoods under our wings and show them the ropes to surviving at Mullen and keeping their dignity whether it worked out in the end for them or not.

And so we kept our distance from many of the white students, which was not hard, since many of them were already afraid of us because of the constant negative media attention pumped into their homes about Five Points. Many of them often linked that same type of media hype to our sagging pants and slang dialect. Ultimately our differences made it a bit easier for both sides to keep a safe distance.

The only white kids who didn't let the flux of constant negative media attention or our appearance keep them in total fear of us seemed to be many of those on our freshman football team. And, at Mullen, football was the name of the game, no matter what color you were or what part of the city you were from. Mullen's football team was considered one of the perennial powerhouse teams throughout the state of Colorado—loved by many, feared by others. The majority of the football positions on the varsity that called for sound athletic ability—running back, receiver, and defensive back—were dominated by black upperclassmen who had been brought into the school. Many of the bigger suburban white players were left to do most of the blocking. It was a lethal combination that worked well then, and still does to this day.

"Having black players at all the fast positions is the only way Mullen can compete," one of our coaches explained.

I went out for football. The game was pretty new to me, and I was placed in the running back position, a position that required rapid thinking and the constant fending off of savage tacklers who tried to take my head off on every play. I had to do a lot of learning.

"Tommy, run through the damn hole," Coach Harper, our freshman head football coach, constantly screamed during practice and games, nearly causing an earthquake, as he jumped up and down and slammed his hat to the ground. "If you're going to be able to play this game, son, you got to run through the freaking hole!"

But it just didn't make much sense to me. The concept of running through a tiny hole in a mesh of massive linemen was one thing that would take a while for me to buy into. And so, I would give my same tired response, "All right, coach. I see what you're saying. I'll do it next time."

When I got tackled by the opponent because I hadn't been able to make it to the sidelines for refuge or to run out of bounds, a fight usually ensued. From the bottom of the pile I'd yell, "Man, get the hell up off of me!" while I rained out punches and kicks. In my mind, I couldn't help but take it personally when someone collared me and dragged me to the ground in a mad rage, and then pounced on me while shouting in victory to his comrades about how great he was.

As the season progressed and I started to trust and grasp Coach Harper's concept that the shortest distance between two points was a straight line, I began to run through the holes, allowing myself to score touchdown after touchdown. But the fights on the field continued. Slowly and subconsciously, football and its on-the-field violence became a way for me to vent and release some of my internal frustrations, hurts, and pains from the past. By the end of the season, the Mullen Mustangs freshman football team finished number one in our conference.

Each day, our journey to Mullen began at 6:30 am when Bobby and I caught the first of our three buses. There was always a tired wait for the #28 bus, then a short sprint to the #30 bus, which always seemed to simultaneously pull off with the arrival of the #28 in downtown Denver, and then one last grueling transfer to the #36 bus that dropped us off in front of the school by 8:00 am. And, after school, engaging in the same process going back home was even more tiresome, landing us at our front door between the hours of 7:00 and 10:00 at night, depending upon the time football or basketball practice let out. Wow, what a long day!

By November of that year, the cold winter chill had settled upon the city of Denver. It had been months since I had been to my former second home, the Glenarm. I walked through the front doors into the sound of running and screaming kids everywhere, pool balls clacking against one another, the laughter of the old timers in an intense game of chess, the enchanting ringing of winning points from the video games, and the smell of sweat that misted the air from the gym. There's no place like the home.

"Waaaatson, what's up? We haven't seen you in a while. How are things going out there at your new school?" Coach Maxey shouted from behind the desk, shining with his same smile.

"It's all right. Our freshman football team finished the year first in our conference, and now I'm trying to get ready for basketball. Man, had I known about all the homework they be giving at Mullen, my decision for high schools may have been different."

"Aw, man, don't worry about that. Once you're done with school out there, you'll be able to go to college anywhere you want to, which will be an opportunity that many guys down here won't get and probably wouldn't take advantage of even if they had the chance."

"Yeah, I hear you," I said, still not convinced or able to picture in my mind what the impact of graduating from Mullen High School would do for me.

"Well, I'm about to go in here and lift some weights. I'll talk to you later," I finished, ending our cheerful greeting and heading for the weight room.

My entry into the hallway near the weight room brought me to a congested doorway of drooling onlookers outside the railing of the weight room. Each one seemed to be "ooing" and "ahhing" about events taking place in the weight room. *What in the hell is going on here?* After squeezing through the group of male bystanders, it didn't take me long to break the code of their fascination.

"Man, she dissed the hell out of you," one from the crowd of onlookers laughed out at the "wanna-be mack daddy" exiting from the weight room, head dropped in a disappointed fashion. Just as I suspected, all the hype had to be over some female who was working out in the weight room.

When I finally made it all the way through the crowd and into the area to begin my workout, it didn't take long to discover that the excitement was, indeed, legitimate. Wow! There she was in the back of the weight room, running on the treadmill and wearing an outfit that fit her like a gentle stream pouring down the enchanted walls of an hourglass. Wow! She was definitely all that and then some, but, at the same time, I wasn't about to be foolish enough to have my name added to the list of fallen "wanna-be mack daddy" victims who got turned away by the goddess.

With my good sense and the odds against me, I figured it would behoove me to keep my mouth shut, work out, and head back home—not to mention the fact that I still suffered from a bit of the childhood "shy-guy" syndrome. Seeing my non-muscular frame in the mirror was a sure sign that I had a long way to go with the weights.

After I had worked out for about an hour, and the hype from the hallway had dispersed, I found myself in a very peculiar situation.

"Hi. My name is Samantha," the figure said, standing above me as I looked up from the bench press station. I almost dropped the weight on myself.

" Hi ... uhm, uhm, Tom ... uhm, I mean Tommy. I mean my name is Tommy," I nervously replied setting the weight down.

And just like that, the floodgates opened for more conversation and laughter, and, a short time later, I was walking with her to her grandmother's house. We walked and talked, talked and walked for what seemed like hours. And I discovered during our conversation that she was only a couple years older than I and a junior at George Washington High School—a high school located in south Denver. I would never have guessed her age from looking at her and listening to her. Both her mind and body were mature far beyond her days, and far beyond mine too.

Our arrival at her grandmother's house brought me to the sudden realization that I had sore feet and no bus fare, and that the walk home would be a long, chilly one.

"Hey, it was nice meeting you," I told her. "I'm about to head on home so I can catch the Penn State football game."

"Don't worry, you can come in and set down and watch the game here," she said, urging me to stay, and blowing away my excuse to try to beat the fading sun and the cold temperature that came with its departure.

But before I could come up with another reason for having to leave— without admitting that I didn't have any bus fare—a voice from behind the screen door of the small, red brick, two-story house called out, "Hi, Samantha. Won't you and your friend come on in and sit down?"

Damn. It's too late to run for the hills now. Doing the only thing that I could do, and reverting back to the words of my childhood training when dealing with older people, I simply responded, "Yes, ma'am." I went in and took my seat, trying to think of a reason to be excited.

Why in the world did I do this? It seemed like the very moment my buns hit the couch, the bells sounded and Samantha's grandma started blasting me with questions nonstop for nearly an hour. "So what are your plans when you get done with school? What is the name of the school you go to? How are your grades? Are you a hard worker? What type of job are you planning on doing later on in life? How long before you expect to get married and have children? And do you think you will be able to take care of my granddaughter and the kids?"

What? Marriage and kids? Did she not know that ninth graders didn't think about stuff like that?

I didn't want to show any visible signs that I was shaken up by her informal interrogation about my future and my life. "Um, I don't know," I responded, giving the same best answer I could find for the majority of her intrusive questioning.

All the while, Samantha seemed to be settling back in total delight, enjoying every minute of this interrogation with a look on her face that said, "Don't worry—she's not going to kill you."

Kill me or not, by the end of our question-and-answer session, I was brain dead and ready to go. "So, honey, would you like some dinner?" Granny finally concluded, with a voice full of innocence and warmth, a contradiction to the previous tone.

*What? Dinner? After all the hell you put me through for the last hour? How in the world can you ask me a question like that?* "Yes, ma'am, I'll take a small bite," I calmly responded.

She made her way to the kitchen, singing the tune of one of the old Negro spirituals. "Oh, oh, oh … Soon and very soon we are going to see the King …"

*Yes! Now I can finally devote my attention to the Penn State football game!* Samantha had turned on the TV before I sat down in that hot seat.

"So, what do you think about what she asked you?" a quiet little voice asked from across the room as I tried to glue my eyes to the tube. *I hoped the little voice would go away.*

"Uhm …" I said.

"What do you think about what she asked you?" the voice said again, showing definite signs that she was looking for an answer.

*Ain't no way I'm about to get caught in no conversation about marriage and kids. Samantha and her Granny are sorely mistaken; they have the wrong man for all of that stuff. But still, there was a plate of food on the way and there was still half a quarter to go in the football game, so saying nothing wouldn't be smart.* "It was okay," I responded, rolling my eyes to the back of my head. *Yeah, right. I hoped that would be sufficient until it was time to go. And it was;* I began to gobble into the huge plate of steamed cabbage and neck bones that had appeared on the tray before me.

With a full stomach and the game over, it was time to hit the road. "Thank you all very much for the food. I'll call you later on tonight, Samantha." *Yeah, right.*

During my walk back home, I realized it was obvious that Samantha was looking for a serious relationship and her granny was looking for wedding bells, lots of grand kids, and family dinners. I was not the man they were looking for, and I wasn't planning on seeing Samantha or her granny ever again in this lifetime. As I continued my long walk back home, looking at the fluffy snowflakes starting to fall from the dark, gray sky, I could do nothing but think about the good night's sleep I was due. *I can't wait to hit the sack.*

However, as soon as I made it through the door and greeted Grandma Louise, the phone rang. "Hello," I answered.

"Hey, Tommy." It was Samantha. "I just made it home. Are you going to come over tonight and meet my parents like you said you would?"

Damn. Of all the things for her to remember from our walk to her granny's house, why did she have to remember the one that I flat-out lied about, trying to impress her before I knew her and Granny's mission? My only defense now was to try and play dumb, acting like I didn't know what she was talking about,

"Um ... what? Meet your parents? I don't know what you're talking about." And, sure enough, she took me back to my exact words—on the exact block, in front of the exact house, and at the exact time. Now she had me on the ropes and I was stuck.

"Um, ummm ... I need to check with my grandmother. Can I ... ah ... get your address and telephone number again and give you a call back?" The excitement in her voice said that this was something she had been looking forward to since the moment I had uttered those foolish words.

I had no intention of asking Grandma, and I had no intention of going to Samantha's house, especially since she lived in Park Hill, a place that now promised imminent harm and danger for people from Five Points. The gang violence between the two communities had sent the city's murder and violent crimes statistics sky rocketing. The newspapers and television stations were constantly bombarding viewers with stories of violent episodes between the rival gangs from the two areas. And it had always been pretty common for guys from my neighborhood to be visiting some fine young lady in Park Hill, since that's where most of them lived. When guys from my neighborhood crossed paths with some of the locals, our guys usually got jumped, hospitalized, and, in some cases, even sent back home in a body bag. Nah, I am not about to be in anyone's Park Hill. Things had changed a lot since I had last lived in Park Hill. Drugs, violence, and gangs had quietly infiltrated the area, which many hadn't thought could ever happen. And, in some cases, the perpetrators from Park Hill were even more notorious than the unruly gang members from Five Points. I remember hearing on the streets and through our local news about an entire family of gang members who lived in Park Hill, having come from Compton, California, being banned from the entire state of Colorado because of gang violence and drug trafficking. I was not going to Park Hill.

After about twenty minutes of thinking about stuff like that, my decision was solidified. And so, the phone started ringing again. I knew exactly who it was, and I wasn't going to answer it. I figured, if I did not answer the phone, Samantha would eventually grow tired and stop calling.

"Don't pay it no mind, Grandma. It's just somebody that I don't want to talk to right now. They'll stop calling," I said politely. But the phone didn't stop ringing; Samantha never grew tired of calling and getting no answer.

By now, Grandma Louise was getting quite irritated and wanted to find out the reason for the calls. I begged her not to answer it, which didn't slow her down a bit as she headed for the phone. I jumped up and took flight to my room, hoping to get myself engaged in some cleaning, which normally took precedence over many other things in the house. Through the ever-so-thin walls in my room, I could hear Grandma Louise greeting Samantha and asking her questions about who she was and why she was calling so much. Her questions drew a prolonged silence by Grandma, followed by several "Um-hum's" and "Is that right?" After she wrote down Samantha's telephone number and other information, she hung up. And I knew exactly where she was headed.

Within seconds, my attempt to suddenly clean my room was rudely interrupted by Grandma Louise, who pushed open my door. She looked prepared for a battle. Her entrance brought about a moment of silence from both of us.

"Did you tell that girl that you would come to her house and meet her parents tonight?" Ouch! The question cut through me like a knife. The question was followed by more silence and that deep stare that only parents and grandparents can give—one eyebrow cocked up and the other setting straight as a board. There was no way I could do anything but tell the truth—plus, she already knew the answer to the question, just as she always knew.

"Well ... yeah, but ..."

And then her hand went up signifying that she didn't need to hear "no mo," as she would say. "But nothing, get yo' stuff on!" What! Get my stuff on?

And that was the end of that. Grandma Louise always felt it was important to be a man of honor. "A real man stays true to his words," she would often say. Despite the fact that it was getting later into the evening, the promise that I made in a half-hearted attempt to impress Samantha earlier now had to be fulfilled.

With my bus schedule in one hand and my bus pass in the other, I was escorted to the door and told to be on the last bus back to Five Points. In silent disgust, I proceeded the rest of the way out the door, after informing Samantha by phone that I was on my way.

Before I knew it, I was at the bus stop waiting for a bus that would take me to Samantha's house. My body shook from a combination of the cold breeze that swept across my face and the horrific thoughts of what might happen if I crossed paths with some of the locals from her neighborhood. And, even though I was not a gang member, just living in or being in an area where they made you fair game to the same torture members were subjected to made me susceptible to the same types of violence.

Once on the bus, I tried to think of a getaway plan to every frightening scenario I could conjure up. I hoped that Samantha was going to meet me at the bus stop as she said she would; that way, I wouldn't have to creep up to people's homes, trying to see if I was at the correct house.

After several minutes on the bus, I finally came to my stop, on 28th and Magnolia. Stepping from the bus onto the partially lit street sent my heart pounding. The darkness produced what looked like lurking shadows in the distance. Seeing a figure emerging toward me from the dark, I stood indecisive, not knowing if I should run off after the bus that had just pulled away or prepare for war. What if it's Samantha? She'll think I'm a punk if I start running. But what if it's not her? What if it's one of the locals coming to put a bullet in my head?

It was pretty obvious by now from my hesitation that I was a foreigner to the neighborhood. In that moment of uncertainty, a voice came from the approaching figure, "Hey, Tommy, I'm glad you made it." It's Samantha! Thank God.

There was no time for small talk. I was ready to get to her house as quickly as possible. Samantha's calm demeanor told me that, either she was oblivious to the things that could happen to us walking down this partially lit street, or she was just used to it.

As we walked, I said nothing, wanting to be as quiet as possible. I mulled over all the stories I had heard from friends—how many of them had been approached by passing cars and people on the streets checking them out to see if they were from the neighborhood. If the locals couldn't get a clear view of you from the darkness, your chances of making it back home that night in one piece were better, but, if they could see that you were not a regular in the area, you were in for a long night. All the stories I had heard from people made me believe that going into Park Hill was like going into Beirut.

With all of these things running through my head, I had no idea what Samantha was saying as we walked the two-block stretch to her house. The side of the street that was partially lit had to be my safe haven to her house—another tactic in staying safe. My actions were the actions of someone walking on a broken bridge, trying to avoid falling into a pit of alligators. During our walk I kept my communication with Samantha to mere grins and slight nods. I didn't want her to hear the nervousness in my voice, and I didn't want the deepness of my voice to bring about any unwarranted attention.

Each car that approached from the distance and passed us with the music blaring sent my heart racing even faster, triggering in my mind my escape route in case one of the vehicles harbored those who didn't want me there. I knew which cars I would hide behind and which fences I would have to jump in an attempt to get to safety if something were to happen. Those were the scariest two blocks I had ever walked.

No sooner did we walk in the door of Samantha's house than I was greeted with handshakes and lots of laughter from her parents. Either they were very happy people or they had just secretly witnessed my paranoid adventure from the bus stop to their home. However, after talking with them for a short time, it was obvious that they were two wonderful people with very bubbly personalities.

The inside of the house was beautiful, each room displaying its own ambiance. The living room, where we stood, was full of bright colors, nice fluffy loveseats, and family photos everywhere. Samantha led me to a table in the corner that held the family's most cherished pictures. First, there was a black-and-white picture of her grandmother from the old days. Next was a photo of her mom and stepfather back when high heels, bell-bottoms, Afros, and butterfly-collared shirts were in style. We moved on to a military photo of her biological dad who lived in another state, and then she went randomly through other photos from her early girlhood and teenage years.

From there it was time to head down to the basement to watch a movie just before I would have to take off to catch the last bus heading back home for the night. As I sat down, I remembered that one of the "special pictures" stood out more than the others to me—the picture Samantha's hand had hurriedly moved past, and the one she had given me no information about. In the photo, a handsome young guy about our age was dressed in a local high school football uniform, holding a football. Why did she move past that picture? And who was the mysterious guy? I wanted to ask her about it, but didn't know how or where to begin. I just let it go.

After thumbing through several videotapes in the wide collection her family had, she picked one and threw it in. To this day, I have no idea what it was about; I was still thinking about that picture. Finally, about a half an hour into the movie, my question blurted out.

"So ... who was that guy in the picture upstairs?"

"What picture?" Her eyes stayed on the television screen.

"The picture of the dude dressed in the football uniform."

This was followed by absolute silence from Samantha, as though I had said nothing. So once again I asked, "Who's the dude in the football picture upstairs?"

I could see by this time that Samantha was becoming a little aggravated by the question, as she moved slightly away from me. And so I became even more persistent.

"The dude in the football uniform, who is he?"

"My ex-boyfriend," she snapped, saying nothing else.

Ex-boyfriend? It seems a bit strange to keep a picture of your ex-boyfriend hanging around like that.

Half-heartedly, trying to pay attention to the movie, I asked a little hesitantly, "So, why did y'all break up?"

"We didn't," she snapped squeezing the remote control in her hand.

What, you didn't? I was completely baffled now and wanted to know more. After a few more minutes of silence, I said, "So how is it possible that he's your ex-boyfriend but y'all never broke up?"

This question seemed to bring about more frustration in Samantha as she tried to ignore the question. She squeezed the remote control even tighter. The silence was now starting to make her appear more standoffish.

At this point, I wasn't sure if I should push the conversation any further or let it go. But there was too big a part of me dying to know how it was possible for the guy to be an "ex" when she'd never broken up with him in the first place. I didn't utter any more words, but I changed my body language. I sat completely erect at the edge of the couch, rubbing my hands together, trying to come up with a follow-up question to find out more about this "ex-boyfriend."

I hoped that, by that time, which was nearly an hour into my visit, it was obvious to Samantha that I was not going to let this thing rest and that I wanted to know more. This brought about an abrupt sigh from her, and she finally turned the television off. "You want to know the story?"

"Without a doubt," I responded.

And so she began by saying how the two of them had been dating each other for a short time. She then went on to say how he was a star athlete for one of the local high schools. As she continued talking, I heard the name "Teddy Williams," and I had a feeling of déjà vu. I knew I had heard the name before, but I couldn't place it, so I continued listening. After giving me just a few basics about their relationship, a couple of tears rolled down her face, and I knew that Samantha was preparing to get to the point of her story.

Where is she going with all of this? I thought to myself.

And so she continued. She began telling me the story of how he was visiting her house one night after he had gotten off from his job at the local McDonald's. Later on that night, he had left her house, riding his bike home. When he was a few blocks from her home, he was approached by a group of gang members riding in a car. This is where I started to remember the name and story, but I had not quite put my finger on all the details yet.

Suddenly the story took a tragic twist, and it dawned on me where and why the story and name were so familiar.

"And that was it," she said breaking completely into tears of sorrow.

Teddy had been gunned down and left to die in the streets, mistaken for a rival gang member because of the color of the hat he was wearing—his hat from work. This was the tragic incident about a star high school athlete killed as a result of gang violence that had been plastered all over the newspaper and television news in Denver just a few months earlier.

The room Samantha and I were sitting in had become dead silent except for the rapid pounding of my heart and the sobbing of Samantha. I was completely stunned at hearing that same story again, and even more stunned to know that he had just come from her house when it had happened. Man, not only was he killed, he was coming from here! I had definitely opened up a can of worms that didn't need to be opened for either of us. By this time, I was in tears, too, saddened by the incident and now even more frightened about my journey back home.

The fear I felt traveling those two blocks back to the bus stop on my way home was twenty times the fear I had felt on my way to her house. Now that was the scariest two blocks I have ever walked. I finally made it home that night safely, but it would be some time before the memory of the tragedy would escape from my mind.

Samantha and I continued to date each other for a while, but later broke up on good terms and went our separate ways.

At the start of my second year at Mullen, I often sat back and reflected about the previous summer and how I had tried to come up with every excuse that I could find to leave Mullen and attend a public school in the neighborhood. I told Grandma Louise that I didn't like Mullen because it had been an all-boys school my first year; that excuse was blown out of the water when Mullen decided to go co-ed in my second year. The other excuse was that it was too hard academically. That didn't hold up either; Mullen created an additional class to provide academic help for those students who didn't have the initial academic skills to survive at Mullen. It was called the De la Salle Class.

What Grandma didn't understand—and what the administration at Mullen didn't understand—was that many of us who traveled from the inner cities to this white suburban school each day had to live in two separate worlds on a daily basis.

On one side, we had to deal with the white kids' fear of us because we were from Five Points and their televisions at home were often flooded with stories of the gangs, drugs, violence, and poverty there. I recall one incident where my coach told a couple of the white players on our football team to give Bobby and me a ride home after one of our long practices that ended late in the evening. It was quite embarrassing and painful to see the white boys literally passing the buck as they tried to avoid having to take us home. "Hey, bud, I can't go down there. Larry, I'll give you twenty dollars if you take them." The twenty-dollar bill went from one white dude's hand to another; no one would take it. I often found it ironic how they were so scared to take us home, but loved our presence on the football field when we aided them in destroying other teams. We eventually got a ride downtown that night from my boy Des, who lived in the suburbs with many of them. It didn't feel good having to undergo situations like this, but still I kept my mouth shut and said nothing about the way I felt, which was something I had learned to do very well from my childhood.

On the flip side, we had to return to our neighborhood and face constant questioning about why we were going "out" to the white school. Some people from the neighborhood saw us as "sell outs" for putting Mullen's sports program on the map and not creating strong teams in the local public high schools in the neighborhood. "Man, y'all ain't nothing but some Uncle Toms for going out there to the white school." This was the sentiment expressed by some of the locals in the neighborhood—or "the 'hood," as we called it.

On the weekends, Bobby and I would go to local parties in our neighborhood and find ourselves holding up the walls as watched everyone else hi-five and yell out and greet each other with the names of their high schools—Manual, East, and Montbello were the names of the schools chanted throughout the jam-packed house parties and nightclubs.

Each day we were torn between these two worlds, and the weight of maintaining our existence in both was just additional stress to carry … one more thing to think about each day.

Ultimately, I valued Grandma Louise and Coach Levine's advice and stayed at Mullen. Coach Levine even turned down a job to coach football at a major Division I school because he wanted to keep his promise to see that many of us from the inner city had an opportunity to graduate. They both talked about the fact that it would pay off some day. If and when that was going to happen, I had no idea. And so life in these two worlds went on.

Stealing lunch food from the school cafeteria became a way of life in my second year of school. Many of us couldn't afford to bring a lunch every day, and we certainly couldn't pay for school lunch every day. The days of free lunches in the public schools were over. I never quite knew the exact reasons or circumstances of some of the other black students who took part in this thievery, but for me there was only so far that Grandma Louise could stretch the little bit of money we had, and I was not going to burden her with yet another expense.

Taking ham-and-cheese sandwiches became a joint effort for all of us from the neighborhood, both upper- and underclassmen. It would start with my boy Troy, who was one of the cafeteria workers. As the other students gathered in the long line to wait for their turn to buy lunch, about six of us would spread out among them—from near the beginning of the line all the way to the back of the line, where one of us stood carrying the bag to hoist the sandwiches in.

"Ya'll ready?" Troy would say, and, once everyone was comfortably snuggled discreetly throughout the line, the process would begin.

The first sandwiches went from the hands of Troy to the person assigned nearest him. And then the sandwiches proceeded down the line. We'd slide them on the floor, tuck them under an arm pit, shove them down our pants, pass them quietly behind our backs—and, finally, they'd end up in the bag waiting at the end of the line. The process did not stop until each of the fifteen black students who now attended Mullen and sat at our table had a sandwich. The black students who didn't take part in the stealing on one particular day played Robin Hood on the following day.

As time went on, many of the white students caught on to what we were doing, and, for the most part, never said a word. Many of them seemed fully aware of the unspoken law, "Never bite the hand that feeds another man." In fact, later on during the school year, many of them joined us in getting free lunches for themselves—not because they had to, but as a way of rebelling against their parents.

"You see, dude, my parents don't have a damn clue what I do or who I am. They just shower me with money, hoping that the mighty dollar will somehow guide me through life," one of the white students expressed to me one day. I guess life in the suburbs isn't always the perfect world many of us living in the inner cities perceive it to be.

"How many you got?" the watchmen at the table would whisper to the bagman. And, when he had enough, he'd give the signal and we'd all fall out of line to eat our meals. Once we had our sandwiches, we would pool our change together for sodas, or borrow from some of our affluent white teammates, which was most often the case. It took some time, but school administrators finally caught on to the huge amount of profit they were losing each week from missing food, and so they brought about an end to our "food drives."

The only alternative for many of us was to bring leftovers from home. The entire lunchroom reeked from the smell of collard greens, chicken, pork chops, chitlins, hot sauce, macaroni and cheese, and anything else we could manage to carry in our plastic grocery bags to school.

With this new year also came an opportunity to play on the varsity football team. This was a huge accomplishment because Mullen's varsity football team was known and respected throughout the state of Colorado.

"Son, listen hear. If you're going to play this game and be successful at it, you can't be punching and kicking people every time someone grabs you and tackles you! You'll cost us the whole game. You're going to have to start using your head," Coach Levine bluntly expressed to me at the beginning of the football season.

If I planned on playing, my attitude toward fighting people on the football field was going to have to change. It was either learn how to play within the rules of the game, or sit on the bench and not play. Because football was becoming a tool for me to unconsciously unleash a lot of the frustration and pain that still ran through my veins, I decided that I would learn how to punish people within the confines of the game. My mission was to punish my opponent with my shoulder pads as often as I could, and as hard as I could, and still get a couple of punches and kicks in whenever the coaches and referees were not looking.

Football was starting to become more and more a part of my future, and my teammates were like my extended family. We went to war together every Friday night, and only the strong survived—and oftentimes we were the survivors. The high that I got from playing football and being on a highly visible and respected team was the same feeling that I had yearned for in my attempt to join a gang when I was in third grade. Moreover, by the end of the season, I had received my first letter of interest from a college. It was from the University of Texas A&M. My future in football was starting to show a glimpse of promise.

Meanwhile, in Five Points, the surge of gangs continued sweeping through the community like a massive tidal wave, engulfing males and females of all ages. For some, it was the thing to do; for others, it was a way of surviving and being a part of something in the public schools if you weren't an athlete. Many of my friends from junior high, who had pledged not to join in on gang activity, had now done so. Based on the options I know they saw before them in school, I can't say that I blamed them. Many of them didn't have the required grades to any longer be involved in formal sports. The Glenarm had increased their membership fees and changed the guidelines for entering into the building. They had been forced to do so for safety reasons—they didn't want weapons being brought into the center. If you were planning to survive the everyday peer pressures of high school in the 'hood, becoming a gang member seemed like a good move. Nevertheless, joining a gang would become a choice that many would later regret.

"Man, look at them crackheads over there looking for that rock," Kevin, one of our neighborhood newcomers to the school boldly said, as we got off the bus after our long ride back to Five Points from school one evening. His comments sparked laughter and additional jokes and comments from the group.

"Man, you better watch out, because they will steal yo' dirty underwear off yo' butt just to get money to buy some crack."

Groups of crack addicts could be found on many of the corners in Five Points, waving and flagging down cars of passersby who seemed interested in paying money for sex or exchanging drugs for stolen goods. From sunup to sundown, this was their mode of operation. "Yeah, man, that's all them crackheads do all day long."

I was slow to speak and laugh at the bombardment of jokes that continued as we walked. Focusing my eyes in on the group of addicts, I could see in the middle a familiar face—the face of my childhood hero, my sister Melony, who had become a full-blown crack addict. With a final look of confirmation, I dropped my backpack and bolted across the street, dodging traffic. My eyes filled with tears of joy and sorrow as I engulfed Melony with the biggest hug and kiss that I could conjure up.

"Sis, how have you been?"

"I am doing fine, little bro, how about you? I hear you playing football now and doing pretty good with it."

"Yeah, I'm okay," I nonchalantly said, trying to shift the focus off of me. After a few minutes of small talk with her, it was time to hit the road.

"Sis', be careful out here, it's dangerous."

"I will, little bro'. Love you," she concluded going back to business as usual.

"I love you too," I responded, boldly walking back across the streets to join my friends who were standing with their mouths hanging. Witnessing what I had just done left my comrades breathless.

"Man, are you crazy?" one of them asked in great surprise. "What the hell you doing running up and hugging a crackhead?"

"Crazy? Yep, I'm crazy only for my family. That crackhead you talking about is my sister, so that better be the last of them crackhead jokes." I expressed myself sternly to the group and kept on walking with my head high. Never again would I ever fail to reveal my relationship with a fallen loved one to my friends, as I had done with Grandma Mae. "Yep, that's my sister."

Melony had always been a rock and warrior for me when we were growing up, and she had also been the same thing to the rest of my siblings. When we were kids, she had been the one who had comforted us when we were scared in the middle of the night when Mom and Dad were not around. She was the one who had prepared what little bit of food she could find in the bare cabinets and refrigerator when Mom and Dad did not come home. She was the one who had to protect us from neighborhood and school bullies. She was the one who had to wipe away our tears when we were missing Mom and

Dad. She was the one who had encouraged us to go to school while she sat with Carmen when my parents wouldn't come home for days. She was the one who never had a shoulder to cry on. She was the one who had no one to encourage her not to drop out of school in middle school. She was the one who had no one to listen to her ideas and dreams as a kid. She was the one who had no one to talk to during her times of trouble and pain. She was the one who didn't have any one to defend her from the sex-driven drunk bastards at Grandma Mae's house. She was the one who had to grow up way before her time. She was the one who kept us sane when everything around us was insane. She was, and will forever be, my hero.

# Chapter V

## *Standing Here Alone—Part 2*

"Boy, what in the world did I just do with them keys? They was just in my hands a minute ago."

"They're right here in the refrigerator, Grandma—the same place where you misplaced them at a couple of days ago."

"Boy, I must be losing my mind around here," Grandma Louise finished, shaking her head in total disbelief.

The disbelief she had about her sudden memory lapse was one that we all shared. Even the doctors couldn't provide a clear explanation to her and Aunt Milly during their frantic visits to the local clinic.

"Momma, these here doctors get paid all this money just to tell you to go home and get some rest. Everything will be all right. It's gotta be something else going on."

But who exactly was right? Aunt Milly seemed to have heard from a great source—her continuously gossiping friend Pauline—that Grandma might be experiencing "the old people's disease" or Alzheimer's, a word and disease many of us common folk in the neighborhood had never heard of.

Each day of my second year at Mullen seemed to bring about more and more odd behavior and conversations from Grandma Louise. "Where is Poppa? I said where is Poppa? I gotta find Poppa, right now!" she would yell late in the midnight hour, standing at our front door in her nightgown, searching for a man who had been deceased since her childhood.

"Grandma, what are you talking about? Come on back in here and lie down," I'd hesitantly say, hoping the neighbors had not heard the outbreak.

As time went on and the episodes continued, I started to find myself more and more in a daze, looking at Grandma, waiting—waiting for the moment one day when she would shake off her recent strange behaviors and say, "Boy, what you doing? Get in there and clean them dishes and tell yo' sistah and brotah ta help ya." When that moment would come, I had not a clue. All I know is that I will be here with you when it does happen.

With another football season winding down at Mullen, I found myself standing in the slushy field of Alameda High School in the midst of a pouring rainstorm.

"Man, I can't believe Coach had us come out here and play in this kind of weather," I said in despair to a couple of my close friends who were joining me in playing in the sophomore football game against Alameda's junior varsity football team. Though we were all freshman and sophomores in school, we had spent our entire year of football playing on the varsity football team at Mullen—playing against the big boys.

"Man, I can't believe this stuff either," they agreed. "But, since we have to be out here, we might as well go on out there and put it on those trash-talking white boys," was the group consensus.

Moments earlier, when the five of us—the only blacks on our sophomore team—had made our entrance into the stadium, it had all begun.

"Nigger, I got some chicken for ya'll over here."

"You stanking niggers and ya'lls nigger-loving teammates are going down."

"You niggers come to the wrong place today."

And these were just a few comments from the parents of our opponents! The players' words were far worse. Nevertheless, Coach Levine always told us that you could never let people like that get to you. So we had a game to play.

On the first play from scrimmage—Bam!—my boy Emmitt took it to the house, scoring an eighty-yard touchdown without being touched! Emmitt later went on to play football for the University of Notre Dame.

"Now what you got to say, chump?" Emmitt joyfully said, tossing the ball to our out-of-breath opponents.

Next series, our quarterback Clements hit our player Brandon over the middle. Off he went to score a seventy-yard touchdown. Clements went on to play football for the University of Miami, and Brandon went on to play for the University of California.

The next time we got the ball, Clements hit our tight end Jimmy for a long ball for another touchdown. We were kicking butt. Jimmy later played football for Duke University.

Alameda had the ball in their third play of the game. Our linebacker Chester delivered a crushing blow, creating a fumble, and allowing Dillion, our cornerback, a chance to pick the ball up for another score. Yes! Chester went on to play football for the University of Arizona, and Dillion played for the University of Hawaii.

Again we had another score with Clements hitting Shane, our tall, lanky receiver. Shane went on to play football for the University of Illinois.

Down the sidelines went Alex, our fastest receiver, for yet another score. Alex went on to play football for the University of Northern Arizona.

"All right, Bobby, come on. Let's take it to the house!" my heroic teammates and I urged. And Bobby did just that, galloping sixty-five yards for the touchdown that ended the second quarter. Bobby went on to play football at the University of Northern Colorado.

Before he led us back out onto the field, Coach Murphy gave us his final speech: "All right gentlemen, I want you all to stay focused. Because you all know teams start to play out of desperation when they are being humiliated. We don't want no injuries," We knew he was implying that the boys from Alameda might try playing dirty in the second half.

"Touchdown for the Mullen Mustangs!" blared—again—from the loudspeakers in the stadium. Our defensive end Clark gave in to a celebration dance. Clark went on to play football for the University of Stanford.

Time and time again we scored, and our opponents remained scoreless.

Coach Murphy took a time out: "All right gentlemen, the game is almost over. We're kicking the snot out of these guys, but they're starting to take too many cheap shots at you guys, and Coach Levin would kill me if any of you got hurt. Here's the deal—Clements, you hand Tommy the ball on the next play. Tommy, I want you to just take a knee and down the ball so we can end the game and go home." He'd had to yell his instructions over the rumbling thunder, and he pushed us back onto the field.

What? Down the ball? Coach must be crazy—I'm about to get me another touchdown when I get this ball.

No one else knew of my plan but Bobby. "I'm about to score on this play, so block yo' defender," I whispered to him.

"Man, what the hell you talking about—didn't you hear what Coach said?"

"I don't give a damn what Coach said, block yo' damn man!" And I pushed him through the muddy field to line up for the final play.

"Down. Set. Hike!" Clements yelled out through drenching rain that was now so heavy I could barely see the other team.

Clements executed a nonchalant hand-off and the ball came to me. I'm sure Clements believed I'd down the ball and the game would be over. Yeah, right! And off I went to the shouts of my teammates, "Tommy, what are you doing? Down the ball!"

"Get him!" was the yell from the opponents.

I was really about to show them now, as I plowed through the sticky mud trying to keep my footing.

I could see a hat-slamming Coach Murphy in my peripheral vision, but that was still not enough to stop me. *I have to show these punks what we're really all about!* I scrambled to turn the slippery corner, eluding diving defenders as I ran. I could see the light at the end of the tunnel as I shifted past a couple more defenders. I was truly about to finish the game on a good note when suddenly I found myself sliding. In fact, only one foot was sliding. The other remained planted, stuck in a mud hole. It was too late to down the ball now. I really had myself in a jam. And, before I knew it, my body was rolled over backwards by what seemed like all eleven of the defenders from the opposing team. With each impact, my head was pushed back closer toward my foot, which was held fast in the mud. I was in excruciating pain. The words "Down the ball, Tommy!" seemed wiser by the second. Back and back I went, until, finally, the pressure of the pileup on top of me and the awkward position of my "stuck" ankle were too much. I heard an awful snap, and I knew my ankle was broken. I couldn't believe it.

"Take that, nigger," the defenders cheered, to the hail of my cries of pain. "Yeah, that'll teach you, nigger."

And teach me it did. Each night I had to agonize through the pain of a broken ankle and the pain of Coach Levin's lectures on humility and selflessness—lectures that I wouldn't hold fast to until years had gone by. The pain in my ankle would eventually go away, but the lessons of Coach Levin would last forever.

Each month brought more downhill changes in Grandma Louise's health, and life at home continued to become more and more difficult. We all knew what the possible ramifications would be for Carmen, Martin, and I if Grandma had to be placed in a nursing home. Aunt Milly's three daughters were now older, and the three bedrooms that had housed us as kids were jam-packed at best. She would have room to take in only Carmen. For Martin and I, the consequences of Grandma going into a nursing home could be grave; it could possibly mean that we would end up back in the system—

back in the crisis centers, and maybe a foster home if there were any takers brave enough to take on two teenage boys.

"Don't worry," Aunt Milly constantly assured us. "Momma can no longer take care of herself or ya'll, so here's what we are going to start doing—during the nighttime you and Martin are going to be responsible for watching her, making sure she doesn't leave the house and wander off down the streets. Carmen can stay with me. And, during the daytime, I'll come and watch after her until ya'll get home from school."

This was the game plan we followed to a tee each day, leaving Grandma's poor health a secret to all of the outside world. Martin and I would take turns throughout the night listening intently for the next random moment when Grandma would end up at the door in an attempt to wander down the dangerous streets of Five Points during the middle of the night to find Poppa. Saying nothing to school administrators or the outside world, we learned to master our plan.

Despite all of our efforts, however, we knew the big question would have to be answered sooner or later. At what point is enough enough? When would we find that we must place Grandma Louise into a nursing home? With all of this uncertainty on the horizon, the dysfunctional family in apartment B on 27th and Marion continued to find every way possible to keep on functioning. Each day became a cause for more holding on and hoping that things would not spiral out of control any further.

And then came more bad news. Suddenly the front door abruptly came flying open one evening. It was a shaken Martin. He immediately took flight to his room. Now what? I thought to myself rushing back to his room to find out what was wrong.

By the time I arrived in Martin's bedroom, he was already in tears.

"What's wrong?" I said, and got no response.

"Martin, I said what is wrong!"

"Its Grandma Mae," he responded, still sobbing.

"What about her?"

"Melony just told me that she's in the hospital, and she might not make it out," he concluded, leaving me speechless. What? Grandma Mae in the hospital about to die? You have to be joking.

He was not joking at all. We went immediately to the hospital to find an unconscious Grandma Mae clinging to a life-support machine. Her eyes were slightly open and were yellow as the morning sun from the poison in her body. Her liver had failed as a result of her many years of alcoholism. Her body lay motionless while her chest mildly rose up and down with the ticking of the machine. Tubes and IVs stretched from her face and arms—the doctors' tried to provide more support and an optimistic ending. But it would be an optimistic ending that would never come, as Grandma Mae died later that same night. I couldn't believe it. Heavily saddened by this tragic event, I could do nothing but sob on the outside, while on the inside I pondered the questions: Why? How? Why does my life have to be like this? How can I have hope when all around me is hopelessness? How do I continue to rise out of bed each morning when my emotions are telling me to get under the bed and escape from all the problems? These were such big questions for a gigantic world that seemed to be eating me alive each day. Still, all I knew to do was to continue doing what I had been doing for the vast majority of my life, which was to find a way—any way—to "stand strong."

The battle scars of life's tragic events in the lives of my siblings and I were starting to take a toll on each of us. Outwardly, the behaviors of Martin were showing more signs of years of frustration. By the end of the school year, he had been kicked out of several local high schools for fighting and being a tyrant. Martin was no longer interested in being involved in athletics, and more and more he started to drift toward the ruthless lifestyle of gangs. This was a piece of reality that I was hard-pressed to believe; I was living in a pit of self-denial.

Losing Martin to the world of gangs made me feel that I had somehow failed—failed to be a better role model and protector for him. He had been stripped from my bosom; our eternal bond had been severed.

All of Martin's life he had been told to be like his big brother—play football like your big brother, walk like your big brother, talk like your big brother, and go to Mullen like your big brother. He grew up hearing these words so much that now the last person on earth he wanted to be like was his big brother.

My unwillingness to totally accept the fact that he was a gang member caused many furious feuds between us. "Cuz, I am about to go to the sto'. You want something?" Martin asked one day, calling me the name used by the local gang members toward one another."

"I said, don't call me "cuz."

"Cuz, you acting real stupid right about now."

"If I have to tell you one more time not to call me that, I am going to put your head through that wall."

And with those words, the fight was on, carrying us out into the middle of the streets in full view of our neighbors. Back and forth we went delivering blows to each other, our swearing echoing throughout the block. The fight lasted for several long minutes, until finally Martin escaped from my grip, picked up a brick, and lunged at me. The brick missed my head by inches, and he took flight into the street. I sat on the ground, stunned. He really tried to hit me in the head with that brick! I couldn't believe it.

Our pain had now run so deep that we were willing to partake in fights against one another with no boundaries. But it never used to be like this. Despite the escalation of our battles, I still had great love for him, and a little voice inside of me served as a constant reminder that he had joined the gang for the same reason I had joined the sports teams. We both sought a feeling of belonging; we both wanted to be a part of something greater than our low self-esteem could carry us.

The one thing that did bring Martin and me together in agreement was Carmen. We demanded that she be in Aunt Milly's house at a certain time. There was no way that she would be allowed to date boys, and we wouldn't allow them to call the house. She was our little sister, and we were going to protect her from all hurt and harm. These were the rules for her at Grandma Louise's house and at Aunt Milly's house. It was almost as if Aunt Milly knew and respected our effort to protect Carmen, giving us free will to discipline her, with the exception of whipping her. She was not going to feel the pain we were feeling.

With all the pressure and turmoil in my life, my mind felt at times as though I were going to lose it and go crazy. The fear of being like Mom and Dad was strong enough for me to push and drive just a little more each day toward a destination that I couldn't even name.

Silence was my greatest protector from the outside world, but later would become my greatest enemy. As long as no one knew about my life at home, I appeared to be just another teenager trotting through the normal years of change that most teens have to undertake.

In my junior year at Mullen, I was one of the major contributors to a dominating football team that was now ranked nationally, and was the top school in the state of Colorado. The letters from the major colleges looking to recruit me for football poured in: Florida, Nebraska, Colorado, Texas, Oregon, Washington, Montana, Oklahoma, Arkansas, and Louisiana, and more. Football, my outlet for release, was starting to look better and better each day.

In the classroom, my struggles continued, more so in the subject of English than in my other classes. My new English teacher, Sister Marie, seemed obsessed with having us read, which was not a huge problem for me until it came time to reading aloud. It seemed that every time, with very few exceptions, I would end up tripping and stumbling through my portion of reading, leading to a room full of laughter and one angry Sister Marie.

"Mr. Watson, do you think this is some kind of joke?" she constantly asked during my moments of superficial laughter with the rest of my classmates as I tried to make light of the incomprehensive mess I made of reading aloud. "If you don't learn how to read, young man, you are going to have a hard time making it in this world."

Just as it had been in my elementary school days, the words on the page never appeared to remain stable. I would say words that looked similar to those on the page, and I would see other words and letters backwards. But there would be no letting up for Sister Marie; she kept having me read in front of the class. So I learned to improve my reading in front of the class by scanning ahead of time through all the words in the section from which I would be reading, familiarizing myself with nearly every word and letter. And it worked. Still baffled as to why I had to resort to such measures to make it through school, I continued to squeak my way through.

By the winter, our household size increased tremendously as Dad and his two younger brothers, all of whom had just returned from prison, had come unannounced to live with us. Grandma Louise was now staying full time with Aunt Milly, providing much-needed space in her former apartment.

The drugs and alcohol of the streets of Five Points had never once infiltrated our household before the arrival of our three newcomers. But, Dad soon started to retreat back to his old friend heroin. Uncle Westly, dad's next youngest brother, continued his daily assault on Wild Irish Rose, Thunder Bird, Night Train, and any other cheap liquor he and his wino buddies could manage to panhandle change for. Uncle Shakir, dad's youngest brother, and a prison-turned Muslim, soaked up the habits of both Dad and Uncle Westly. Needless to say, we were back living in chaos.

Several months following the arrival of these three, our household was bestowed with another surprising arrival. Martin's now heavier-than-ever affiliation with his gang had provided him the opportunity to cross paths with a blast from the past. He met up with a person who was also in the gang, but who resided in a different section of the city—our older brother Levi. It was a thrill seeing him again after being separated for all the years. I couldn't believe it. At six foot five and 270 pounds, he didn't look much different than he had when we had last seen him in the hallway of Ms. Mary's house—just a bit bigger.

"Levi, what's up, man? How have you been doing?" I was ecstatic that first time he arrived at our apartment with Martin.

"Just chillin'" he responded back.

"Man, we got to hang out together. Maybe me, you, and Martin can all go hang out at that new club everybody been talking about."

"What? Hang out? With you? Martin told me that you're one of them "preppy boys." I don't kick it with no preps. If you ain't part of my gang, I can't roll with you. Ain't that right, M-tin?" he concluded, reaching over to perform the gang ritual handshake with Martin.

"That's right, we can't be seen with no preps—it'll cramp our style," Martin boasted, leading Levi off to his room. "Come on, big bro. Let me sho' you our room." It was painful—a slap in the face to be treated like this by Levi.

The weeks following Levi's arrival would become even more challenging and disheartening as Dad, Uncle Wesley, and Uncle Shakir all started to buy into the notion that I was a "preppy." Uncle Wesley and Uncle Shakir would find daily reasons to start in on me when I refused to loan them any of the $20 Aunt Milly sometimes gave me so I could have a little spending money for myself.

"Yeah, you think you all that because you go to school out there with all them white folks," they would say. "You ain't about nothing. And you ain't never going to be nothing." Day in and day out, this became their routine. Sadly, both of them would later pass away from cirrhosis of the liver, caused by alcohol.

Now that Dad was back, he felt it necessary to play the role of "big, bad dad." "Y'all going to do some cleaning up around here today," he would say in his best big, bad dad voice, but his commands fell on deaf ears. It didn't take long for him to see that his bullying and controlling tactics were not working any more, especially with me. Inside I carried years of anger and hatred toward him. The beatings he had bestowed on Mom and his lack of responsibility as a father fueled my distaste and lukewarm enthusiasm for him.

Since I was the most resistant, Dad saw me as a threat—because I could deter Martin and Levi from lending him money for his drug habit. "I wouldn't give him anything; he ain't going to pay y'all back," I told them when Dad stood before them with his hand out. His eyes burned with anger as he looked at me. He knew there was no way I was ever going to bow down to him again. "Is that right? Well, you ain't going to be nothing, little nigga. You ain't nothing but an Uncle Tom, who is going to be laughed at when you don't make it out there with them white folks. You ain't going to amount to nothing, white boy," he responded with anger.

These comments were painful, and the effects continued to jar my self-esteem. With a smile and my usual retort of "whatever," life went on.

During the day, while Martin, Levi, and I were at school, our house became a shooting gallery for the many heroin addicts who hung out with

Dad. In the evening, it became a crack cocaine preparation center for both Levi and Martin, who were selling drugs. And then there were all the women we had coming and going to and from the house. Whether or not Aunt Milly knew about all of these happenings was not clear, but what was clear was that it was way too much for one person to monitor or control. All the things that Grandma Louise had told us to avoid had now spilled into our world. "Now, you see that boy over there? Y'all don't hang out with him 'cause he's in them gangs and selling them drugs. And them girls setting over yonder? They ain't going to amount to much, walking around half dressed." These had been the things Grandma wanted to protect us from as she conducted her ethics classes from the window.

My opportunity to establish a more solid relationship with Martin and Levi came during spring break of my junior year at Mullen. Days earlier, Martin had been jumped and beaten up by a family of guys from our neighborhood. Levi, Martin, and even I vowed for revenge.

One day our opportunity came. "There that punk go right there," I said to myself seeing Kevin, one of the main perpetrators of Martin's beating zoom past me on his bike appearing to be headed for either his girlfriend's house or grandmother's house—both lived nearby. This would be the day for payback.

The dilemma Martin and I now faced was going into the fight alone, because Levi had been sentenced to ten days in jail for parole violation one day earlier. It don't really matter because I am the big brother of this family. *The onus was now on me to redeem matters.*

"Martin, Martin," I yelled, racing through our front door. "I just saw one of them punks who jumped you. He's headed up the street."

Nothing else needed to be said as the two of us scrambled back to our rooms to throw on T-shirts, shorts, and tennis shoes—practical clothing for a fight on a warm Colorado spring day.

"All right, Martin, you ready?"

"Just one more thing, and we'll be set," he said running back to his room. "Yep, just one more thing ..."

When Martin arrived back to the living room, he had it with him—his chromed, pocket-size twenty-two automatic gun. Damn! This was a sure sign that this might be a fight like none other I had entered into before. Was I ready for a fight like this, where someone could get seriously hurt or killed? Was I ready to see my little brother shoot someone and spend the rest of his life locked up in jail? But the other side of me was saying that we had to do something. And we had to have something with us just in case we got outnumbered in this battle.

"Hold up," I said, just before we headed out the door. "Give me the gun and take the bullets out."

"What? Give you the gun and take the bullets out? You must be crazy."

"I'm dead serious. We going to fight, not kill someone."

"Here," Martin responded, dumping the bullets from the gun to the floor and handing the gun over to me. "Now come on, we got to hurry before he leaves from over there."

We found Kevin's girlfriend's apartment complex buzzing with excitement from the early spring heat wave. Kids were running back and forth playing tag throughout the streets and parking lot. The teenage girls were playing "double Dutch" jump rope in the alley. Music was blaring from several of the apartments, and occupants sat kicked back in chairs on the front porches with their heels propped up on milk crates. *What in the hell are you doing, Tommy?*

And, before I knew it, we were in front of Kevin's girlfriend's porch.

"Where is that punk Kevin at?" I shouted at her in a rage.

Her face went blank seeing me, the neighborhood "athlete," in a light she'd never witnessed before. "He's not here. He's around the corner at his grandma's house!" By this time, many of the other people standing around had stopped what they were doing to see what all the ruckus was about.

"What ya'll want with him?"

"None of yo' damn business?"

With the snap of the finger, Martin and I were headed around the corner to Kevin's grandma's house. Curious bystanders trailed after us. As we ran, I took the gun out of my front pocket and placed it in my back pocket, making it known to everyone that a showdown was about to take place.

"Oh, no! He has a gun!" someone yelled from the crowded complex.

We could hear screams throughout the complex behind us as we turned the corner. *What in the hell are you doing, Tommy?*

As we continued toward Kevin's grandma's house, I glanced at the many scattering faces around me. People were seeking shelter from what could be another neighborhood homicide. *What in the hell are you doing, Tommy? What have you gotten yourself into?*

It was too late for retreat. Before I knew it, I was standing shoulder to shoulder with Martin in front of what seemed like a hundred people who were sitting on Kevin's, grandmother's front porch. Martin stood, holding a brick in his hand behind his back. He shouted to Kevin, "Bring yo' punk ass down here!" Kevin charged at us like a raging bull, and about ten of his family rushed down the stairs toward us as well.

In that instant, everything seemed to turn to slow motion as I pulled the gun from my back pocket and pointed it at Kevin and his charging family members. *What in the hell are you doing, Tommy?* Their faces turned almost white, and each stopped cold in his tracks as he looked down the small barrel of the gun. Screams rained from everywhere on the block. Immediately, Kevin and his comrades began their retreat back to the porch, hoping to take cover. Quickly, Martin launched the brick he had behind his back. It landed dead center in Kevin's back.

The entire block was in an uproar—people at the mortuary across the street ducked behind the hearse, mothers dragged their kids to safety. We could still hear horrified screams from every direction. *What in the hell are you doing, Tommy?*

We ran and ran, and we didn't stop until we entered the safe haven of our apartment. With only minutes to spare, we scrambled through the apartment seeking a hiding place. I couldn't believe it. *What in the hell have I gotten myself into? All I wanted to do was to defend my brothers and establish a better relationship with them!*

That evening and into the night I sat waiting, wondering which would arrive first, the police to haul us off to jail or Kevin and his family with an act of retaliation. By 11:00, everything was still quiet. The entire incident seemed to be a done deal, and I went to bed, hoping tomorrow would hurry up and come so I could forget about the entire ordeal.

At three o'clock in the morning, I was sound asleep. Suddenly, the glass in my bedroom window shattered. What the hell? Someone's trying to break in! Hysterical with fear, I lunged out of bed, and, in that instant, my body fell like a medicine ball to the floor—I was still practically asleep. Scrambling frantically in a crawl, I made it out of the room and into the living room. Everyone else had already been awakened by the noise.

"What is going on back there?" Dad asked, hunched over in the darkness of the living room.

"I don't know. I think someone is trying to come through my window."

Martin grabbed a knife from the kitchen, then he and I quietly followed Dad back to the room to find out what had happened. We stood in complete silence peering at waving curtains in my room. Back and forth they gently blew, sending patches of light here and there from the streetlight outside of the window.

"Shhhh, be quiet," Dad said, continuing to peer through the darkness.

Finally, the coast seemed clear. Dad turned on the light so we could do some further investigating. The moment the light came on, we were all stunned by the breathtaking sight. The curtains still blew softly from the breeze coming through the shattered window, but now we could see that they were laced with shredded holes. The walls above my bed were riveted with bullet holes. The glass in my window was gone, having been peppered with bullets, and the slugs from the bullets were lodged into my closet door on the other side of the room. Man, they were trying to kill me!

A phone call to the police revealed that others on the block, hearing the gun shots, had already called. We waited and waited for the police, who never showed up. As I sat pondering, I knew this had been payback for the events of the previous day with Kevin. The question crossed my mind, Do I let this ride, or do Martin and I mount up and retaliate? I came to my senses and realized clearly that things had gone too far. Things now needed to be left in the hands of the police—whatever that entailed.

"Tommy Watson, please report to the dean's office," came from the loud speaker in my Spanish class, waking me from my Monday morning daze in school.

When I reached the dean's office, I was notified that I had a call on line one.

"Hello?"

"Tommy, this is Aunt Milly. I got bad news."

"Bad news, what are you talking about?"

"Those boys your brother Martin has been having problems with tried to jump him again today in school. Martin brought a gun to school with him. He met up with the boys in the lunchroom and tried to shoot them. He's now in the custody of the Denver Police."

"What? Are you sure?"

"I am sure. The school just called me and it's been the breaking story on the television the entire morning." I couldn't believe it. All of this had now snowballed to a much bigger problem.

If he was tried as an adult, Martin faced the possibility of two counts of attempted murder and more than sixty years in prison. Fortunately, he pleaded guilty to a lesser charge as a juvenile, and was sentenced to fives years in juvenile prison. The guilt I felt for my part in keeping the situation going haunted me for years. And the question of how I could have better responded to things came to visit me in the late hours of every night that followed. I couldn't believe how things had turned out.

Whether I liked it or not, Martin was not going to be around for some time. Soon after Martin's conviction, Mom was released from prison and vowed to turn her life around. She, too, agonized from the guilt of not being able to come to the aid of Martin in his time of need. "I'm going to be here for you guys," she said constantly. This promise seemed to be different from her other promises from the past. Neither Dad nor drugs would be the apple of her eye now. Thank God. Plus she had now established a relationship with God, which had been something she had been working on since going back to prison.

With Grandma Louise finally in a nursing home where she could receive better care, Mom's timing was perfect.

Mom still needed time to get back on her feet, so Carmen remained with Aunt Milly for a couple more months. Mom moved Levi and me into a cheap apartment on the corner of 23rd and Clarkson, and she resided in temporary housing for former inmates, also known as a halfway house.

Our apartment on Clarkson was a place crawling with everything from cockroaches to crack addicts; it was the only place Mom could afford to house us. The green-colored walls and the steaming radiator constantly pumping out too much heat made the apartment a difficult place to be in, but I tried to make the best of it. Many times Levi would spend the night at one of his many girlfriends' homes, leaving me to witness alone the constant night action taking place right outside the window. I could hear every drug transaction being made. "Here's a stereo," one of the addicts would say, waiting to get a piece of crack from one of the many dealers roaming around. Sounds of shoot-outs between the local drug dealers echoed through the apartment. "Hey, that's my shit," a voice would yell, as the sound of footsteps running past the window was followed by the sound of continuous gunshots.

Nightly knocks at my door sent me shivering with panic into the kitchen to get a knife for protection. "Hey, I got ten dollars on it," a wired crack addict would yell from the other side of the door. The addicts searched for crack all night like starving rats looking for cheese. "Man, you got the wrong apartment. Don't come back here again," I'd yell through the door, almost letting the words, "… or I'll call the police" slip from my mouth. Calling the police on these folks was a no-no. And letting them know you were calling the police was a major no-no that could cost you your life and get you labeled as a "snitch."

I could clearly hear every door kicked down by SWAT teams entering other apartments on drug busts. "Open up! It's the police," they would yell just before they tore the front door to shreds.

The nights I spent during our two-month stay at 23rd and Clarkson were some of the worst nights I ever spent. On the other hand, my stay there was highlighted by a phone call from the legendary University of Nebraska head Coach Tom Osborn. It would have been interesting to see his expression if he knew the chaos he was phoning into. But hardly anyone knew—not even school officials at Mullen.

Phone calls and letters from major colleges across the country kept me motivated to get up each day in hopes of someday playing in the NFL. When she could track me down, Aunt Milly attempted to give me the college recruiting letters that had been mailed to her address and each message from coaches who had called her house.

"Tommy, you are getting mail from a different college nearly every day, and my phone won't stop ringing with coaches calling wanting to tell you good luck in your senior year and that they'll be keeping a close eye on you and the Mullen Mustangs. Boy, that got to make you feel good. So hang on in there."

It was all good, and, as much as I was hurting on the inside, I refused to show any outward sign of disarray. To many in my family, I appeared to be weathering the storm, strong as a rock.

After she got out of prison, it didn't take long for Mom to see that society was not as forgiving as we were. "I can't find anyone even willing to give me a chance to work," she said, time and time again. It made me angry. Here was a woman trying to do the right thing, but no one would give her a chance. And soon the quick prosperity that drug dealers were able to obtain caught Mom's attention, and selling drugs soon became her way to take care of us. After bouncing around between a couple more places Carmen, Melony, Levi, and I were back living with Mom on 27th and Humboldt.

February 6, 1992, was National Signing Day for scholarships for all high school football players. My academic future looked promising to me as I anticipated my senior year on the football field. I still faced academic struggles in the classroom, but I had several months to get things together before that magical day.

With support from my coach in the classroom and support from Mom in the stands at my games, I could see the light at the end of the tunnel. Letters from colleges continued flowing in by the dozens every week. Many of them were from coaches, while others were from unfamiliar female students attempting to lure me to their universities through seductive letters of enticement.

> Penn State University:
> "Rest assured that we will be following your progress this season, and on the behalf of Coach Paterno and the football staff at Penn State University, we would like to wish you continued success this year."

> Stanford University:
> "We sincerely hope you achieve the high goals you have set for yourself, both in the classroom and football field."

Colorado State University:
"We are proud of our program here at Colorado State and hope that you take a hard look at us."

University of Arizona:
"Our future depends on our ability to recruit student-athletes like you. We hope that you will give us careful consideration as you prepare for your academic and athletic career."

Texas Tech University:
"Only the top players are awarded scholarships in the Southwest Conference. Our coaching staff is very interested in becoming more familiar with you. We look forward to watching you play and getting acquainted with you and your family."

University of Florida:
"Our game will be televised by the ESPN network ... we hope you will have the opportunity to follow the Gators this week for a game we think will be a classic."

University of Hawaii:
"We believe that every individual has the ability and desire to work hard .... We'll help you to reach these goals and create even bigger ones .... Hope to see you in the green and white."

Female college student:
"When are you going to plan to come up for a visit? I can't wait to put a face with a name!"

*Wow! I can't believe it.*

As the season came to a close, our team was undefeated and ranked as high as number eleven nationally, having destroyed most of our opponents with double-digit scores. We played our last game of the regular season in front of a crowd of nearly ten thousand who came out to Mullen Stadium to see us battle against our cross-town rivals Cherry Creek, who were also undefeated and who ranked in the top twenty-five nationally. We were ranked number one in the state, and they were number two. The game promised to be one of the all-time best high school football games ever played in the state.

The dark night sky was full of flying seagulls. The weather was perfect for a fall football game. The sweet smell of fresh popcorn drifted through the stadium. The school buses arrived full of hyped-up students from different schools. More and more spectators arrived, the overflow of cars spilling well down the back road of the stadium. It was all astonishing.

By the end of fourth quarter, to the delight of every fan, the ball game was tied at 20–20. Neither team had dominated at any point during the game. Time was winding down, and we had the ball on our nineteenth yard line. Things appeared to be in our favor. Over the noise from the bands and screaming fans, Coach Levine yelled in the play, "All right, men, we're going to run Z up, 22 H crack back."

This was a play that had worked like magic earlier, enabling Emmitt to score a touchdown in the first quarter. In the play, Emmitt and I lined up on opposite sides of the ball. With the snap of the ball, Emmitt started out running for the sideline, giving me time to come streaking across the field to blindside the person who was guarding him and break Emmitt free to score a touchdown. The only catch to this play was that, if there was a chance I might hit the defender in the back, I had to abort the hit so I wouldn't get a penalty flag. Rarely, if ever, was there no opportunity to get the crushing hit on Emmitt's defender. This block, with only seconds remaining in the game, would give us the victory and the undisputed conference championship title.

With the snap of the ball, my cleats tore into the grass. I gained more and more momentum across the field with each step on my way to deliver the big hit. Dodging defenders as I crossed the field, I came closer and closer, and I bore down on the defender as soon as the opportunity presented itself. Suddenly, I noticed that the nice move Emmitt had put on his defender had left the defender wondering what to do. His back was still turned toward me, so the words *Abort the mission!* Abort the mission! ran through my head. I lunged to avoid contact, missing him by inches. I raised my head up from the grass to see all of our teammates in the end zone heaving a delighted Emmitt up over their shoulders. He had scored the touchdown.

"Yes! We won!" I said to the opposing team player who was lying on the ground near me. "Yeah, right. You see what's on the ground over there?" he responded, pointing to the late flag that had come from the pocket of the official on the sidelines. No way. I couldn't believe it.

This one call on me cost us the ball game, giving the other team a chance to come back and beat us in overtime. That one play seemed to change the entire destiny of our team—and the season. We lost in the early rounds of the playoffs to a team that should have been playing Pee Wee Football. It took me weeks to get over that one incident, and the agony of not knowing how it would affect my recruitment made it even worse. I had so much riding on getting that scholarship to play college football.

But over the next few weeks, I was surprised to see that the play hadn't affected my recruitment at all; several colleges extended invitations to me to visit their campuses so we could mutually explore how well suited we were for each other.

Returning home from school on one of our cold, brisk December days, I found Melony on the couch with her head buried in her lap, sobbing her eyes out. "What's wrong, sis?" I asked, concerned. Getting no response from her, I asked again, with more sternness, "What's wrong, sis?"

"It's Mom," she said, trying to gain her composure.

"Mom? What about her?" My heart was beating so loudly I could barely hear myself talking.

Once again she went silent.

"Melony, what happened to Mom?" I was getting angry.

"She was arrested for selling drugs and is going back to prison."

"What!" *I don't believe this. It's not happening. Not again. This has to be a nightmare.*

And this nightmare was a sad reality from which there was no waking. In the days that followed Mom's arrest, I saw less and less of Melony and Levi. Again, our main concern was Carmen, who had been able to move back in with Aunt Milly. With our December rent paid for, I had a month to come up with a plan for somewhere to live. The alternative was homelessness. The fear of this happening was monstrous. *Where can I go? Who will take me in?*

The instructions Mom sent from prison were simple: sell as many of the items in the house as I could so that I had gas to make it to school and food to eat.

The light at the end of the tunnel had all but gone out. I had no idea what to do or how I was going to survive. Spending the days crying in the bathroom stalls at school and spending the nights crying alone at home made it difficult to distinguish one day from the next. I tried hard to appear to not be in too much distress to Aunt Milly, who was exhausting her food and economic resources on me during the lag time before I'd be able to sell anything from the house.

My girlfriend's pregnancy was additional fuel to keep me going. I couldn't give up. I couldn't give up on the one thing coming into this world who'd love me unconditionally and never leave me. Getting my girlfriend pregnant was intentional on my part; I needed something to love and be loved by, and a baby, I thought, would be the answer.

Staying focused and trying to keep the recruiters believing that I was just another ordinary student-athlete that they were recruiting was becoming more and more of a challenge every day. "So, Tommy, how are you and your family doing?" they would ask during the phone calls to arrange visits for me to come see their college and for them to visit my home. "Oh, everyone is doing just fine, and I look forward to seeing you soon," I concluded with each call, hoping for divine revelation for a plan.

When the college coaches came to my house during this period, they were greeted by either Aunt Milly or Mom's close friend, Angela, who took turns playing the role of my mom. It was almost like a real-life movie, seeing Aunt Milly and Angela put on Oscar-winning performances for the coaches. "Yes, we would love to have Tommy attend your university in the fall. He works hard and would be a big help to your team."

My best friend was the only one who knew my situation. He'd say to me nearly every day, "Man, T, I don't know how in the world you're holding up through all of this." My response was always a half-hearted shoulder shrug. In my mind I had no idea how long I could continue to defy the odds.

I needed something to take my mind off the chaos. Getting a break from my world and hearing about someone else's problems was exactly what I needed when Bobby and I won tickets to see a sneak preview of a new movie called Boyz N the Hood.

Boyz N the Hood was a movie that followed the lives of three boys growing up in South Central Los Angeles. Two of the boys were brothers and the third was a close friend, Tre, who had just moved back into the neighborhood with his dad because his mom felt she could not raise the little boy to become a man. As kids, they got into a little trouble and had to spend some time in juvenile hall. The older of the two brothers, "Doughboy," got into some trouble that was a bit more serious and was locked up until he was eighteen. The younger brother, Ricky, had always stayed involved in sports—football, to be exact—which kept him out of trouble. It was his dream to graduate from high school and then go on to play college football for a major college. But there were two things standing in his way that could have possibly kept his dreams from becoming a reality. One was his struggle to pass the American College Test (ACT), so he could be eligible to receive a scholarship to play college football. The other was a combination of the negative social element in his neighborhood and his brothers' gang involvement.

As time went on, things were looking pretty good for Ricky, and, because of his performance on the football field, he had many major colleges looking to possibly offer him a scholarship, depending upon whether or not he had passed the ACT in his last attempt. Neither he nor his family would know the results for several weeks. Ricky's dad was not in the picture, his mom was addicted to drugs, and he and his older brother's relationship was not too close because they had grown up in different places—or households, if you want to call jail a household.

Ricky was admired by many of the locals in the neighborhood for his involvement with football. His neighborhood was full of gangs, so, because he was an athlete with a chance to go to college on a scholarship, he was not the norm in the neighborhood. This also made it difficult at times for him to fit in with the other kids. Despite not fitting into the norm of the neighborhood, he still tried to hang out at the local "hot spots" sometimes to stay in the loop with his brother and old friends. Sometimes this meant he was in the wrong place at the wrong time. But this didn't concern him much because Doughboy and his gang were always around for his protection, and, besides, he felt that he would soon be headed to college and then on to the pros.

One day at the local hangout, Ricky bumped into a group of guys who were from a rival gang of his brother's gang. But, Doughboy was there and saw that a confrontation was about to take place. He and his gang rushed to Ricky's rescue. The situation was quickly defused when Doughboy pulled out a gun and asked if there was a problem. With a gun pointed at them, the members of the other gang said there was no problem—but in the back of their minds, of course, they were thinking about revenge.

Weeks after the incident, Ricky was coming out of a store with his best friend, drinking a carton of milk, and just talking with his friend and having a good time. Suddenly, a car full of guys pulled up alongside them—the guys he'd had an altercation with a few weeks before were back and seeking revenge. The chase was on, and Ricky ran through the alley and jumped a couple of fences in an attempt to get away, but it was too late. They caught up with him and shot him in the chest. In seconds he was dead. Everything that he had hoped for and worked so hard for was gone. He had fallen victim to one of the barriers in his path—the societal element. As for the academic barrier, passing the ACT, his family found out that same day he was killed that he had passed the test. It was indeed too late. What a shame.

Our exit from the movie theater brought a hush of silence over the two of us, as well as over the hundreds of other diehards who had hoped for a happy conclusion to the story. The ride home in my 1978 Fleetwood Cadillac was one that was filled with stillness. I just kept thinking to myself, *This has to be the best movie I have ever seen.* But how could it be such a great flick? It had ended so unexpected, so prematurely, and so violently. It seemed so real. A chill came over me when I realized that the movie I had just watched was almost a direct reflection of my own life and situation. It wasn't long before I was driving down the street in tears.

Bobby must have been thinking the same thing because he, too, broke down in tears. This was the first time that either of us had seen the other cry outside of a sporting event. "Man, T, that was yo' life. You got to be careful," he said, as if it might be the last opportunity he'd have to tell me. Thinking about the end result for Ricky in the movie only created more tears and uncertainty.

The silence in the car was broken when we said out loud that we loved each other, and then quickly vowed not to talk with anyone about the tears we had shared. We decided that, for the sake of our manly reputations, we should keep the details of the events in the car to ourselves. We hadn't yet learned that a big part of manhood is being able to cry and refurbish the soul in moments when it is needed. The sadness about what I had seen in Boyz N the Hood would be with me for sometime.

# Chapter VI

## *Trying To Face Another Day—Part 2*

Colorado State University hosted my first college football recruitment visit. I was wowed by the beauty of the campus. The brute mountains made a gorgeous backdrop for the school's massive, historic buildings that were home to resident halls and classrooms. The sidewalks were full of people retreating home after a long week of school.

My weekend visit was to not go beyond the forty-eight hours required by the NCAA. Could this be a possible engagement party for CSU and me? I didn't know for sure, but I was eager to see what she had to offer. With this visit also came the opportunity to meet about twenty-five other top high school athletes from across the country who were also exploring the idea of a long-term courtship with CSU. We all had a chance to meet some of the instructors and administrators who told us about several academic tracks that we could possibly pursue if we became students at the school, most of which fell upon deaf ears. We were there for football and more football, which especially seemed to be the case for several of CSU's football players who remained sound asleep in the back during the whole spiel on academics.

Seeing the massive football stadium and athletic dorm made me realize that the difference between college sports and high school sports was like the difference between night and day. That difference even became more obvious as we explored the nightlife of the city and saw the attention generated from the mere sight of an athlete at the local bars.

At each local hangout, it was the same thing. All heads turned when we walked in— nearly fifty of us athletes, all equipped with our secondary greatness attitude and all needing to be recognized socially for our talents. We were led to the front of the long, winding line and granted free admission. We checked out all the seductive, whispering females. "Man, we got it pretty good around here," one of the older players whispered to me as we wove our way through the crowd. "This happens all the time." I couldn't believe it. It was like heaven on earth.

Once we were inside the smoke-filled club, the females packed around us, looking as eager as race horses at the starting gate—eager for a chance to hang out with the team of players for the night. I can bear witness that many females who wouldn't even have given me a second glance in my early high school days, now wanted my complete attention. "Can I have this next dance?" each of them attempted to ask in her most seductive voice over the loud music. "Maybe later," I'd respond, repeatedly trying to feel things out. Alcohol, of course, saturated the club; the smell was all pervading. Nearly every face in the place was glued to a bottle of beer, including that of many of my fellow recruits.

"Tommy, what's up? What you drinking tonight?" My host Big Greg asked me.

"Man, I don't drink alcohol, but I'll take an orange juice mixed with pineapple juice." A little surprised, Greg yelled my order across the bar. Big Greg seemed to respect my decision not to drink alcohol, which was the case with nearly all the football players from the team but one.

"You know what, little bro'? I came in here just like you," Big Teddy said, guzzling from a beer. He held another beer in his other hand and still tried to bob his six foot six, 290-pound frame to the music that was blaring through the club. "You see, I came here on my visit and I said the same exact thing, but then I tried a little brew and now I love it."

"Nah, man, I don't mess around with that stuff," I said, trying to keep him from falling right over on top of me. After we went back and forth a few more minutes, Big Teddy finally got the point and stumbled into the corner behind the huge speakers, where he remained the rest of the night, laid out in his puke.

As the night wore on, the place became more crowded. The number of females approaching the athletes with their telephone numbers and drink offers was amazing and continued throughout the evening. Before long, I was having the time of my life on the dance floor, with my shirt off, leading the universal house party chant, "The roof, the roof, the roof is on fire, we don't need no water ..."

By Sunday morning breakfast at Head Coach Earl Bruce's home—the final outing for all of us recruits before going back home—I was sold on CSU, and CSU appeared to be sold on me. "Tommy, we at CSU really want you to be a part of our team next year. And, if you're interested, we have a scholarship that we want to offer to you." Yes!

On Monday, when I arrived back at school, I notified Coach Levin that CSU was the school for me, and that I was ready to notify the media of my oral commitment. Coach Levin, being the intelligent man that he was, simply asked, "So tell me what you discovered about CSU outside of the fact that it was a fun place to party."

"Uhm … uhm … Well they got … ah, ah. I mean I learned … ah … ah," was the only thing that seemed to come out of my mouth. Not a word as to what they could offer me long term.

"Do you know how CSU ranks against other schools that are recruiting you?" Once again my response was the same. By the end of our one-sided conversation, I totally got the point he was making about finding out about the academics that were offered as well as venturing out and seeing what lay beyond the state lines of Colorado. Coach Levin, in his wisdom and compassion for me, knew that staying in the confines of Colorado wouldn't be good for me. I figured I would take his advice and make the visit scheduled for the following weekend to Texas Christian University (TCU).

Not only was this going to be my first time in Texas, but it was also my first trip on an airplane, which I hadn't been looking forward to.

"Tommy, your chances of getting into a car crash are greater than your chances of getting into a plane crash," my teacher Mr. Wallace assured me. My logic told me that I would rather get into four car accidents and suffer broken bones than to get into that one fatal plane crash.

Despite my fears of flying, the flight to Texas went smoothly. I arrived at the Dallas/Fort Worth Airport in heady anticipation. I wondered if the hospitality and masses of black people would be as surprising to me as it had been for other people I knew who had traveled down south. My journey to the South also brought back memories of the stories Dad had told about the prejudice of whites there. Each glance from a white person during my ride to the hotel created paranoia inside me. I wondered if they were all calling me a nigger. Luckily for me, the excitement of traveling soon gobbled up this paranoia.

I felt great comfort from the large number of TCU players standing before me in the lobby of the hotel with their hands extended, saying, "Welcome to Texas" in their heavy southern accents. Texas was hospitable, and there were masses of blacks, based on what I had seen so far.

Once we were situated in our rooms, it was off to the campus to meet more players and see the facilities. Nearly all of the high school recruits that I had the chance to meet were from Texas. This told me that Texas was such a huge state that it did not really need to have anything to do with the rest of the country. The environment and setup of the athletic dorms was not much different from that at CSU in the sense that the football players lived exclusively as one big family, separated from regular students. The players did just about everything together—everything, that was, but party together. The white players on the team went to their parties and the black players went to theirs. This pattern was the norm on most campuses that I visited. In fact, beyond knowing about each other's hometowns and a few high school football stats, black players and white players really didn't seem to know much about each other. Like many of the other players, I thought nothing of it at the time, and my white high school teammate, who was also being recruited by TCU, and I said our good-byes, knowing we would see each other at the end of the trip.

Later on that night as we all gathered in the football players' dorm rooms before going out to a party to be put on by one of the black fraternities in town, everyone sat around laughing and joking while cases of beer circulated among the fifty to sixty of us. I remember thinking that this drinking must be some universal thing that went on among all teams before going out. Everyone on the team was talking about how they couldn't wait to get to the party. I had no idea what a fraternity party was like, but the one thing I did know was that, if it was anything like the parties at CSU, I was all for it. "Man, I am going to get about twenty honeys tonight," one the players shouted across the jam- packed room. "Man, you ain't going to do nothing but sit in a corner and jack off," another player shouted back to everyone's laughter.

Just like at CSU, when the alcohol came around to me, I gave my spiel about how I didn't drink alcohol and passed it on to the recruit sitting next to me. Standing before me was Big V, as some of the players called him—six foot eight, 270 pounds, muscles bulging everywhere. He held in his hands two forty-ounce bottles of Old English beer.

"Come here, little bro." He motioned me to follow him into the hallway. "I was just like you when I came here on my visit. Until I tried it, I never knew what I was missing. Now I drink all the time," he slurred, leaning unsteadily against the wall. He wiped the drool from his mouth, waiting for me to respond.

"Man, I don't mess around with that stuff because of my own personal reasons," I said, as humbly as I could.

"Well, you don't know what you're missing out on," Big V concluded, stumbling back into the room. I stood thinking for a moment that either Big V and Big Teddy, from CSU, were distant relatives or every campus in the country harbored someone like the two of them, who chose to succumb to the peer pressure and then take on the role of advocate to get others to follow in their shoes. By the time I got back to the room, Big V had already passed out on the bed, where he lay for the rest of the night. It was too bad that he missed the party because it was off the hook—one of the best parties I had ever attended. Being at this party landed me the opportunity to see some of the most beautiful black women I had ever seen in my life. Just as the women had at CSU, they jammed in long lines hoping to catch an evening with one of the football players. Little did I know at the time that this type of out-of-control partying on my college trips would be the genesis of the wedge that would later come between my girlfriend and me.

By the end of the visit, I was sold on TCU. The Fort Worth Star-Telegram newspaper read "TCU lands versatile player from Colorado."

After that visit, I canceled all remaining visits to other schools and was able to boast to Coach Levin about TCU's high graduation rate for its players, which wasn't really that big a deal to me since my plan was to enter into the NFL draft as an underclassman.

Back at home, I still had the scary reality of homelessness looming over my head. My only chance was to graduate from high school and go to college.

Aunt Milly worked around the clock trying to find housing options for me. "Tommy, I haven't found anything yet, but you hang in there and keep praying. Aunty is going to find you somewhere to stay." The sad reality that there were not many people willing to house a near-adult teenager was tough to get around. Somehow I had to stay focused and move ahead.

One evening while I was sitting at home watching television, I heard a bunch of confusion in front of the house. The sound of police sirens and cars screeching to a halt and doors slamming indicated that whatever must have been going on outside had to be close. When I ran out the front door, I was immediately greeted by the pointed guns of the Denver Police Department. The cops had Levi spread out on the hood of his car. "Go back in the house," one of the officers ordered, gun in hand pointed at me.

Later on that night, Levi called from jail. He wanted me to go outside and look alongside the house to see if the police had recovered a bag of crack cocaine that he had thrown there during the chase. To my surprise, it was still there. When I got back to the phone and Levi asked, "Well, was it there or not?" in a moment of hesitation I responded, "No ... uhm ... it's not there anymore."

"Damn," he responded, and hung up.

The next day I called up Bobby to see if he knew anything about selling drugs. Not long after the phone call, Bobby and I were in the kitchen prepping the crack to be sold. The money from drugs would surely put some money in my pocket until things stabilized for me.

Bobby and I began prepping and selling the drugs on a daily basis. One day, while we were at my house prepping the crack in the kitchen, the doorbell rang, surprising us both.

"Damn, who could that be?" I said quietly.

"Maybe it's the police," Bobby jokingly said.

"Funny ha-ha. If it is the police, you will be the one going to jail, since the stuff is in your hand."

I opened up the door and in popped the last person on earth that I wanted to see at that moment—Aunt Milly. "Oh, oh ... hi, Aunt Milly," I said loud enough hoping Bobby would hear me. Streams of sweat poured down my forehead.

"Boy, why you looking like that? And who's back there in the kitchen?" she asked, heading for the kitchen.

My stomach dropped to the floor; I didn't know what to say, and I didn't know how to stop her from heading into the kitchen where Bobby and I had been prepping the drugs. Each step she took made my heart pound harder. I can't believe this! I was dying on the inside at the very thought of seeing how disappointed she was going to be to discover that the nephew she was trying so hard to help was selling drugs. *Lord, please don't let her see the drugs. I'll never sell them again if you help me.* As she continued walking, the only thing I could do was prepare to explain to her why I was engaged in such an act of stupidity as selling drugs.

"Bobby, what are you doing here?" she asked, once she arrived to the kitchen. Preparing myself for the next question, I just dropped my head hoping that my explanation would be enough to buy back her forgiveness. To my surprise, Bobby had thrown all the pots in the sink and put the crack in his pocket just before Aunt Milly stepped into the kitchen. Jokingly she said, "What were y'all doing back here, using drugs or something?" By now Bobby was sweating like a man getting ready to enter the ring with Mike Tyson.

"No, we ... ah ... ah ... were just talking about school," I managed to squeeze out of my mouth.

"Well, I just come to tell you that I found somewhere for you to stay until you graduate from school." With my heart still pounding heavily it didn't even dawn on me until later what she had said. That close encounter with Aunt Milly and the possibility of the great disappointment—along with recognizing the feelings of guilt that I had already been experiencing from taking money from drug addict parents who didn't even bother trying to feed their children—brought about an abrupt end to my selling drugs. That night, the drugs went in the trash, and I vowed to myself that I would never do anything like that ever again.

Days later, I took the offer of Ozzie, the man who would later take Aunt Milly's heart and hand in matrimony, to sleep on his living room floor until I graduated from high school. His timing was perfect. I escaped to his house with the mattress from my twin bed and as many clothes as I could fit into the trunk of my car—just days before everything in the house was once again tossed into the front yard. I had been seventy-two hours way from homelessness. Saved by the bell—and Aunt Milly.

Shortly after my trip to TCU, my decision to verbally commit to the school was challenged when notification came stating that TCU head coach Jim Wacker had accepted the head coaching job at the University of Minnesota. This posed a dilemma for me. I loved the very idea of attending school in the warm south, but Coach Wacker and his great energy had been one of the major reasons that I had chosen TCU in the first place. The ironic thing about this was that I had always thrown University of Minnesota recruitment letters away following the whipping the University of Colorado had put on the school earlier in the year. But, after a trip to the University of Minnesota and experiencing the same thing that I had experienced at the other colleges, I recanted my verbal commitment to TCU and made a new one to the University of Minnesota. But my covenant with the University of Minnesota would not become official until the February 6 signing, which was still weeks away. I also still had to graduate from high school, which was going to be a long shot. I never thought the same recruiting process that started off with such excitement would leave me so drained.

My new temporary spot with Ozzie was ideal. It was about twenty minutes from Five Points, giving me a chance to get away from all the hustle and bustle. The apartment was a quiet one-bedroom where I occupied the living room floor. The other thing that I had brought with me from my previous location was my cherished collection of collegiate letters—one letter from each of the colleges that was recruiting me.

Once I was settled in my temporary place of shelter, the clock began ticking and it became even more important that I stay focused on my schoolwork, basketball, which was something that colleges wanted to see— the dual-sport athlete—and spending as much time as I could with my girlfriend. Because I didn't have a back-up plan in place if I didn't graduate, I saw my next four months as a do-or-die situation. The struggle to graduate was intense—so intense that I had to make arrangements with my chemistry teacher. In order to pass the class, I had to go in and do extra work before school, after school, and at lunchtime every day in addition to my regular scheduled class period. I knew what was waiting for me on the horizon if I didn't graduate and receive my scholarship, so I accepted my agreement to this class with open arms and total gratitude.

On the basketball court, I was known for being a pretty ferocious defender, which became another, however lesser, avenue for me to unleash some of my frustration. In the final quarter of a game at our rival school's gym, we played a long, hard-fought game. I was the star of the battle, and the opposing crowd was giving me hell every opportunity they had. Many of the opposing folks sitting in the stands had also been stadium "hell raisers" for their football team, to which we had suffered a controversial defeat earlier during football season. By the fourth quarter, the constant heckling had taken a toll on me mentally. Each time I stepped to the free-throw line to shoot, the place erupted into an uproar as the fans chanted, "Watson sucks, Watson sucks, Watson sucks …" And on and on it continued.

After each of my shots, I stood at the free-throw line, giving the "hell raisers" a bird's eye view of my mighty middle fingers. Take that, bastards!

"Now, Watson, I have already warned you several times about doing that. The next time, you're out of the game," the referee said, yelling over the crowd, who loved every minute of his rebukes to me.

"Well, you need to tell them that all the stuff they're saying ain't necessary," I said arguing back before my last shot.

"Watson, just play ball."

Each and every opportunity Bobby and I got to hammer Cherry Creek's key players we delivered. We delivered elbows to the face, ribs, stomach, back, and anywhere else we could slide some pounding in without catching the eyes of the referees, all the while hoping our coach would understand our frustration with the crowd and forgive us later.

"What in the hell is wrong with you two? You're acting like a couple of thugs out there," Coach Thomas, our head basketball coach, yelled at the two of us in the huddle during our last time-out. "You two have to get control of yourselves so we can win this game and get the hell out of here."

But not even his pep talk could keep us from going down. We went down and went down hard, defeated by a double-digit margin.

Following the loss, we had to endure the long ride home from the city of Cherry Creek, a place that not many blacks frequented. As we tried to leave the area, we found we were being tailed by a carload of hell raisers, who annoyingly blew their horn at our vehicle for blocks. They leaned out the car windows, yelling and heckling—it was clear that they were having a good time. That's it! I've had enough.

"Look! Them bastards are flipping us off. Let's show them what's up," Bobby yelled. It sounded like a marvelous idea to me, so I hopped out the passenger door of the car at the red light, where I was immediately greeted by one of the "hell raisers," who stood well above six feet and neared the 300-pound mark. He had to be one of their football players. Surprisingly, he knew my name.

"Come on, Watson, you want a piece of me?" he barked, provoking support from his cowardly comrades who were still in the vehicle. With that statement, I prepared for war, bobbing and weaving my way closer and closer. Suddenly, when I was close enough, "wham!" I got him right dead smack in the middle of his face, almost sending him to the ground. Not wanting any more, he took off running around the car, trying to get his comrades to let him back into the locked vehicle. I ran after him, taking the pole from Bobby, who stood stunned by my rage.

"Hey, bud, I'm sorry," the hell raiser repeatedly said, as I continued chasing him in a circle around the vehicle with the pole. I had lost it, and my pursuit seemed to last for an eternity. That was, until the police cars arrived.

The police drew their guns on all of us, and detained us, leaving the fight to go no further. And, during my cooling-off period, I could do nothing but shake my head in great disappointment at my actions. I had let the game and the heckling get the best of me. If I would be privileged enough to go on and play collegiate sports, I would need to get used to this type of behavior from crowds. We were fortunate to get a break that night, and scurried back home with complete gratitude.

After weeks of non-stop plugging away at the books, it was time to get out and have a little bit of fun. And what better place to have some fun than Denver's annual Martin Luther King, Jr., Day March, which remains to this day one of the largest in the country. All week long, the media had been reporting the big question, "Will the Ku Klux Klan rally, taking place at the same time and place of the MLK march, disrupt the march for peace?" Great question. Denver's first black mayor of the city, Wellington Webb, attempted to follow each of the media reports of the KKK's presence with a statement of peace, encouraging marchers to stay focused on the "true" purpose of the day and not to give in to violence.

The beautiful early morning blue skies hovered over the crowd of tens of thousands gathered at City Park for the march. The crowd was a mixture of students, elders, doctors, lawyers, parents, small children, whites, blacks, gang members, drug dealers, and just regular civilians. This was the one day that always brought everyone together no matter which neighborhood they lived in, no matter what gang they were in, no matter how much or how little education they had, and no matter their color.

The KKK would be holding their rally at the same place the MLK March concluded—downtown at the Capital. MLK marchers would finish off the march and rally to hear speeches from community members who had both direct and indirect experience with the civil rights movement. It was no secret to any of the marchers what we would encounter once the march entered into downtown.

In his concluding remarks to the crowd that was nearing twenty thousand, Mayor Webb reminded us to ignore the other rally going on downtown and stay focused on what we were about, which was nonviolence. Following those words, the sea of bodies poured into the streets of Colfax Avenue, en route for our destination. The army of people seemed to stretch for miles. Throughout the crowd, many sang old Negro hymns, while there seemed to be a silent hush among others—mainly the younger people—as if they were reserving energy for something big.

Our route went past jam-packed sidewalks of spectators. Feeling some of the tension of the young people, many of the older community members filtered throughout the crowd to try to keep people focused on the notion of nonviolence. "Come on, sing it now, '… we shall overcome …,'" an older gentleman sang, trying to engage the participants behind us to sing along with the group in front of us. The hymn "We shall Overcome," was like a whisper in the dark falling upon deaf ears for many of us "youngsters," as they called us. The overcoming that we were preparing for was having the KKK "overcome" the butt kicking we were about to bestow upon them. "It's on when we get down there," several youngsters whispered, and passed the message along.

As the march poured into downtown Denver, it became very obvious just how divided the crowd of marchers was. "Let's do this," was the cry that swept over much of the crowd as many tied bandanas over their faces and removed their coats in preparation for war with the KKK.

"Y'all gotta ignore them folks," was the last-minute plea coming from many of the older people who had stopped and were trying to encourage the marchers to keep walking past the capital building. Their pleas were unsuccessful, and, within minutes, nearly half of the crowd of marchers had broken off and were at the bottom of the stairs of the capitol building. The KKK stood at the top of the stairs. Creating a barrier between the two groups was what seemed like the entire Denver Police Department.

Rocks and bottles flew toward the cowardly Klansmen, but landed short of their targets since no one had the arm strength of John Elway, former quarterback for the Denver Broncos, to throw anything three hundred yards. The crowd became more and more unruly and instantly began to unleash its frustration on the police. A bottle came flying from somewhere in the crowd, striking one of the officers in the face. This sounded the bell for the rest of the melee to begin. The entire line of police officers was showered with rocks, bottles, snowballs, pool balls, and anything else people could get their hands on there or had brought with them. And, before long, officers were going down left and right with injuries as the crowd continued to pour on the pressure to break the line of policemen. Seeing the police for once in this type of submissive position seemed to be payback for many of the unruly attackers. They were glad to see the police getting a dose of their own medicine.

Then, out of nowhere, a canister of tear gas came flying into the crowd, creating a moment of panic for people near it, until one youthful white marcher picked it up and tossed it back into the line of police, who were putting on their riot gear and masks. Seeing this, the KKK had no choice but to retreat into the capitol building for safety.

"We are asking one more time for you to disperse—or you're going to jail," one of the superior officers shouted from a bullhorn, which did nothing but ignite the crowd to launch more objects at him and the other officers. Within minutes, the march for peace had escalated into a full-scale riot. Tear gas canisters filled the air with thick smoke. Rocks and bottles were flying from every direction. And it wasn't long before the mob of people spilled over into the streets headed for the business section of downtown to do some looting. Wow! I was dead smack in the middle of everything. Many of the older marchers tried to counter the chaos with yells, "You all are doing exactly what the KKK wanted you to do." Seeing that their message was not being heard, many could only turn and walk away in tears and disgust.

The rioting and looting seemed to go on for hours. Thousands of people were running in every direction trying to seek refuge from tear gas, bottles, and rocks. Police cars were overturned and set on fire, mailboxes and trash dumpsters were overturned. Pieces of destroyed newspaper stands became the weapons of choice for smashing through the front windows of merchandise stores at the 16th Street Mall. Sirens and screams flooded the air as fire trucks scattered throughout the area fighting dumpster and car fires, and parents tried to find their children. In the midst of all the mayhem, I literally bumped into Uncle J.R.

"Tom, come on, get your butt home before you get hurt or go to jail," he yelled, attempting to pull my arm and make me follow him through an alley filled with innocent people fleeing for safety.

"I'll be all right," I shouted, trying to make my way to the broken window of a Foot Locker store that was flooded with looters. I was on a mission, and a very stupid one at that.

Later on that evening I received phone calls from friends I'd met from my college visits in other states. "What happened at the MLK March in Denver?" was what they all wanted to know. With each explanation, it began to dawn on me just how stupid and insignificant our behavior had been. The older folks had been right; we acted like fools doing exactly what the KKK had hoped for. Seeing innocent civilians and police officers on the news who got hurt only confirmed that thought. Had I gotten arrested or injured, I could have ruined my future—all for a little bit of fun.

# Chapter VII

## *Trying To Stand Strong—Part 2*

February 6, 1992—finally, the national signing date for all high school football players. It was an honor to be part of that elite group of less than three percent of all high school football players each year to receive a scholarship to a Division I school. My full-ride scholarship to play in the Big Ten Conference, which was the toughest college football conference in the country, guaranteed that my entire college career would be completely paid for, as long as I made the necessary grades and graduated from high school. The entire school was filled with exhilaration. Newspaper reporters, cameramen, and photographers filled the principal's office to witness the signing of my letter of intent to play football for the University of Minnesota.

"Son, I'm proud of you, but you know there's a lot more work to be done in the classroom to solidify this deal," Coach Levin whispered to me in the midst of the flashing cameras. "No doubt," I replied, knowing that this was only another step toward my destination to happiness—the NFL.

After months and months and months of hard work, I went on to graduate from Mullen High School, by the skin of my teeth.

Days after graduation it was time to head to Minnesota on the Greyhound bus with everything I owned. On the ride to the bus station, I felt as if I were taking the journey of a man who was saying his last good-byes before heading off to an unknown world. Even in my sad state of mind, I understood why I had to go so soon; the well was starting to run dry of favors that people were willing to do to help me get to a place that was hopefully going to save my life—college. The only reward they were seeking in return was that I "go off to college and become a man and do something with myself." But how … how was I to become a man when I had never really had a chance to be a child?

As I looked out from my seat on the bus, tears filled my eyes and sadness overwhelmed my heart. *What if I don't make it?* If I didn't make it, everything that folks had done for me would have been in vain, and all of the negative events and thoughts would become self-fulfilling prophesies. *There's so much pressure and so little clear guidance toward the direction I must push.*

No one in the world that I was leaving could share the dos and don'ts of college life with me, for they had no idea themselves. Not knowing what to expect with my new life in Minnesota scared me to death on the inside. But, on the outside, my attitude was, "Oh, you know me. I'll be just fine."

Moments earlier, during my ride to the bus station, I had tried to soak in my last look of my neighborhood—The Glenarm, The Pig Ear Stand, City Park, Gilpin Elementary School, Deep Rock Water Company, The Shoe Shine Shop, Safeway Grocery Store, Ethele's Soul Food Restaurant, Sonny Larson Park, and The East Village Apartments. *When will I see it all again?*

The farther and farther my Greyhound ride took me away from the city, the more my eyes became clouded with teardrops, until finally the tears streamed down my face behind my dark sunglasses. I couldn't hold it any more. My head fell onto my chest and I heaved a quiet sob. *What am I going to do? How am I going to do it? And what are the new expectations of me as I head into this new world?*

"Young man, are you okay?" the stranger setting next to me asked.

With a brief nod of yes, I dropped my head and continued sobbing. I quietly cried for nearly fifteen of the twenty-two hours it took to get to Minnesota. Here I was, heading off to college with my mom in prison; my dad in prison; my little brother in prison; Melony strung out on crack roaming the streets of Denver; Levi gangbanging on the streets of Denver; Grandma Louise, my last legal guardian, in a nursing home suffering from Alzheimer's disease; Sheryl in foster care in a distant place; Carmen living with Aunt Milly; and, at the same time, knowing I had a child of my own on the way. And here I sat on the Greyhound, a trunk carrying everything I owned stowed away in the baggage area. I didn't know if there would be a home for me to return to some day.

My arrival in Minnesota brought me not only a pounding headache but also the notion that the only way I was going to survive in this foreign land was by not thinking about or talking about my troubled past to anyone. I had to forget about it and be tough. This was the treaty established for Tommy Watson, signed and sealed by only Tommy Watson. It would be my secret.

"Welcome to Minnesota, Tommy. How was the trip?" Coach P greeted me the moment I stepped from the bus.

"It was fine. I enjoyed the scenery," which was a big fat lie. There had been nothing eye-catching to see all the way from the eastern plains of Colorado to Minnesota.

Coach P had arranged for me to stay with several upperclassmen defensive linemen over the summer until the dorms opened and the rest of the freshman football players arrived in August. It was great that he was able to put this together given the fact that my arrival in Minnesota in May was way earlier than most freshmen were required to report on campus. During our ride to my new temporary place, I noticed that many things in downtown Minneapolis reminded me of home. The sights of homeless people, taxi cabs being driven by foreigners, and teenagers walking around in baggy clothes eased some of my discomfort with Minnesota. In fact, I wore my clothes the same way.

My new home for the summer was the Riverside Apartment Complex, which looked just like the huge high-rise building on the television show Good Times.

When we finally arrived at the player's thirty-second-floor apartment, it didn't take long for me to realize that I was no longer playing high school football. This was big-time ball I had entered into.

"Tommy, you'll be staying here for the summer with Ed, Darrel, and Dole. They'll take good care of you," Coach P said, introducing me to my new gigantic roommates, who stood between six three and six seven, and tipped the scales between 270 and 315 pounds—all solid muscle. My six one, 200-pound frame looked pretty wimpy.

"What's up, little man?" each of them greeted me, nearly crushing my hand.

"You all take good care of my boy," Coach P instructed them, walking out of the apartment. *Wow! These guys are huge.*

It took some time to get used to sleeping on the floor in the living room, which had no curtains and was the first room to be greeted by the 5:30 sunlight each morning.

In my first week of residency in Minnesota, one of the biggest challenges I faced outside of loneliness was learning how to cook. My roommates were very independent and cooked primarily for themselves whenever the urge arose. All my life, even in difficult times, there had been, for the most part, someone there to cook my meals—and when someone wasn't there, I was able to get by on cold cereal, bacon and eggs, and cupcakes.

After I'd been in Minnesota a week, it became evident that eating cold cereal, bacon and eggs, and cupcakes everyday was not enough, especially with the running and weight-lifting regiments that we were doing during summer workouts. I was running short on money, most of which went to buying the phone cards I used to talk to my girlfriend, so now was not the time to be experimenting in the kitchen. The fact that I couldn't cook was not something I wanted to reveal to my roommates; after all, being in college meant being able to be independent.

For the first time, I was hearing terms like "checking account" and "savings account." "I'm going to run over to the bank and take some money out of savings and put into my checking account," my roommates said every time they needed money. In the past, the only places I had seen money stored were Dad's sock, Mom's purse, Grandma Louise's bra, and under Aunt Milly's mattress.

My roommates found it equally strange that I always ironed my clothes on a towel spread out across the floor or couch. "What you doing? Haven't yo' momma and daddy taught you how to use an ironing board?" Dole said one day, before going off to summer class. "Ya'll are some strange folks out there in Colorado," he finished with a chuckle, heading out the door.

Acknowledging these shortcomings in my brief amount of time in Minnesota, I figured it would behoove me to start introducing myself to some of these basics of my new life. I immediately opened up a bank account. Then I added spaghetti to the list of things that I could cook. The habit that would take some time to break would be ironing on the floor; there was just something that seemed taboo in giving that one up.

The next thing I needed was a job, which the athletic department found in no time, getting me a gig at a local potato company. My job of catching and stacking carts of potatoes for eight hours was definitely not what I'd had in mind. And the ride home from work on the bus was just as agonizing, as everyone around me buried their noses into their garments to avoid the reeking rotten potato smell on my clothes.

When I wasn't at my job, working out, or on the phone with my girlfriend, I was downstairs hanging out with the locals at our apartment complex. There was just something about being with the common folks that always excited me. Conversing with the gang members, crack addicts, and the drug dealers about life almost made me feel at home in my new surroundings. "Man, you know you are the only one out of all the University of Minnesota athletes who will even stop and speak to us?" one of them said one day, and many of the others reminded me the same thing on a daily basis. It was funny to hear them talk—and to hear the other blacks on the team talk. Each of us, as blacks, commonly started off so many of our sentences with the word "man." I would later learn that this was a tactic black men began to use toward one another during the civil rights era to counter being called "boy" by whites. But these residents were right—many of my teammates did not seem to show much interest in spending time getting to know them.

Many athletes, like those who played for the Denver Broncos that I had admired on television as a child, avoided small interactions like "hello" or "what's up?" with the locals in their travels as well as at home once they'd "made it." It seemed that some of my fellow athletes were beginning to behave the same way now that they were on their way to stardom. Whether it was right or wrong, those locals, for many of the players, no longer fit the profile of what they saw as "success."

After about a month in Minnesota, having no social life outside of talking to my girlfriend on the phone, I started to hang out with the other players on the team who were returning to Minnesota to get in shape before the season started. The more I hung out, the more I found out about how athletes survive financially and emotionally on college campuses.

"You see, these females around here will do whatever you want because you are an athlete. Man, what you got to do is get yo' self a team of them who will do fo' you in all the areas you need doing. Because, in this world, Tommy, an athlete is 'the man.'" Really? "These females will do whatever you want them to do."

Running short on money, having just quit my job, my curiosity was sparked.

So, after going to a few parties on campus, those words of wisdom from the veteran players on the team started to play themselves out. And I started to build my own support team.

"Now that you're away from home, sweetheart, you're probably going to need someone to help you do some of things Momma ain't here to do. Take my number and call me later." It was that easy. At each party I received three to four of these kinds of invitations. And so my team of females began to grow and grow and grow.

"And this ain't nothing compared to what it's going to be like once football season and the school year starts. Here at the University of Minnesota we have fifty thousand students, and half of them will be trying to get at the football team come this fall. I got females who pay my rent, pay my car note, wash my clothes, clean my place, and give me sex whenever I get ready. And don't think it's just the white females—they come in all colors and shapes." Moon, another veteran, made it plain and simple for me and for several other freshmen who were in town by now, and also learning lessons on how to become a college "playa." "Even if you ain't got no game, you can still have a tight team of females just because you on the football team."

The more and more I got sucked into this new world, the less time I spent on the phone talking to my girlfriend back home. Chasing skirts was becoming my forté.

It blew my mind that I could now call a female up and anything I wanted was mine for the asking. Anything from sex to money—there seemed to be no boundaries. And the best part was that I didn't have to spend much time with any of them, so I didn't have to worry about someone getting too close to me and seeing my wounds. More and more, this type of lifestyle became a way to cover my insecurities and pain. In this world, it was all about who had the best game on the field and who had the most females off the field. I would later discover that many of the females who subjected themselves to this type of behavior had self-esteem just as low and, in most cases even lower, than those of us on the football team. However, we were all able to use sports as a safeguard to protect our insecurities.

My team of females was comprised of young ladies of all colors and shapes, but the one thing that always baffled me about Minnesota was how many of the black men seemed to have very little interest in black females. To that end, many of the black men who dated white women exclusively seemed to have a tendency to tear down black women to justify their reasoning for dating white women, which was a sure sign to me that they were not truly comfortable dating white women, or that they may have had some problems with their own blackness. The problem for me was not about blacks dating whites and vice versa; it was about taking pride in dating whomever you chose to date and not making excuses for your actions. But many of the black men in Minnesota who decided to date white women exclusively never seemed to have the backbone to take that kind of stand. "With white girls, you get the sex and money without the drama. Black girls always going to bring drama," was the common slogan for many of them. Nevertheless, it was what it was, and life went on.

As the summer wore on, more football players returned to Minnesota, and we began to hang out together more and more. Suddenly, I was confronted with a startling question, "Tommy, are you a gang member?"

"What, a gang member? What you talkin' about? I ain't down with no stuff like that, cuz," I snapped back. I guess it didn't help much that my favorite word to say was "cuz" and my favorite piece of music was a newly released rap song by DJ Quik called "It's Just Like Compton." In it, he raps about Denver being just like Compton, California. The reason I listened to the song had less to do with the fact that it mentioned Compton and more to do with the fact that it mentioned Denver. In fact, most Saturday nights I was glued to the television watching Cops, because there was a series that had been taped in Denver. I simply loved my city.

Thinking about the question in the weeks that followed, for the first time, I began to see just how much growing up in a gang-saturated environment had influenced my own tendencies. It was a classic case of, "You can take a person out of the streets, but you can't take the streets out of a person." I would later go on to discover that not being able to take the streets out of a person was not necessarily a bad thing; the problem for many people who grow up on mean streets is that they didn't know how to take what they learn from the mean streets and use it in a constructive manner to better themselves and the people around them.

What many of my teammates saw when they looked at me was a guy who had a fear of wearing red, said the word "cuz" every now and then, and wore pants that sagged to his knees. But this was me—and I was something that many of them would just have to get used to.

By the fall, during our first all-team meeting, the difference between high school and college sports revealed itself even more to me. One hundred and twenty-seven players, each of whom was the cream of the crop in his high school, city, state, and, in some cases, the whole country. This was a major transition from my team of twenty-seven players. The vast majority of the players came from states like Florida, Texas, California, Michigan, Illinois, Ohio, and, of course, Minnesota. Each of us was striving to make it to the next level—the NFL.

The weeks leading up to the start of school were grueling. Practice was twice a day—we called them "two-a-days." The day started at 5:30 am when one of the staff administered a wake-up beating on the door of each player. "Boom, boom, boom!" I'd be startled out of sleep. Then I'd hear a loud, deep voice yelling, "Wake uuuuup!" And so it went down the hallway. This sort of awakening always brought back many horrifying memories of waking out of my sleep in a panic.

As a team, we operated by what we called "football time." If we had to be on the field to run by 6:00 am, and we arrived at 6:00 am, we were late. On time in the world of college football was being ten to fifteen minutes early. Being late didn't happen very often once we experienced the consequence—a thousand yards of "up-downs"—jogging in place, falling to the ground, and jumping right back up for one thousand yards. I needed only one dose to keep me on time. I had to do them on several other occasions for skipping class, but never again for being late.

After a full day of practicing twice a day for two hours, one hour of lifting weights, three hours of watching practice films, a couple hours of free time, dinner, and a snack before bed, we welcomed our 10:30 pm "lights out." We knew tomorrow would be even more intense.

My freshman roommate Don—or "Do-Do Wat" as he preferred to be called—was a wild Cajun from the Big Easy, New Orleans. Like me, he also had attended a private Catholic high school. Do-Do Wat was what some would call a six one, 185-pound "cock strong" defensive back. His bench press of nearly 400 pounds surpassed mine by leaps and bounds. Lifting weights had not been my strong suit in high school. Do-Do Wat was truly the energy of our team—I don't know whether we all laughed more at his jokes that we didn't understand or at his unusual laugh, one that could be heard all the way across the dorm.

There wasn't a day that went by that my man Do-Do Wat wasn't reminiscing about his grandmother's gumbo. "Say, Bruh, I can't wait 'til she come up cher for a game, so I can sho' you some good eatin'," he'd say in a heavy Southern drawl. We got along well together and granted each other mutual respect, which was not the case for all new teammates. Some players bickered back and forth about everything—space in the room, the telephone, and who snored the loudest.

The University of Minnesota was the second largest university in the country, with a student enrollment of nearly fifty thousand students, which made my old high school of 700 students look like a small family. In fact, during my first year of classes, one of my classes topped off at an even 900 students. And being in a class of this magnitude provided great training ground for skipping classes—at least until I got enough of doing up-downs!

In the beginning of our two-a-day practices, many of us freshman were taught a valuable lesson in surviving the world of college athletics when some of us decided to go exploring the city during our two-and-a-half-hour rest break in the middle of the day. "Man, ya'll better go back to the dorm and get some rest before the next practice," one of a group of seniors urged a group of us freshman as we waited to catch the bus downtown. "Aw, man, ya'll just some old worn out men. We'll be all right," one of us answered. We laughed in great confidence.

"Okay, but ya'll are going to learn to take advantage of the recovery time," the senior concluded, and headed back to the dorm.

Later on that afternoon, many of us freshman almost passed out trying to get through our two-hour grueling practice. Our bodies were drained as we battled fatigue and dehydration from the scorching August sun. That's all it took for us to regard the advice of the more experienced players, who were now becoming like older brothers to us. From that day on, we learned to take full advantage of our recovery time, getting every ounce of sleep we could get between our demanding practices.

Another important lesson we learned from the seniors was that, with this type of training at the collegiate level, our bodies were going to hurt and hurt bad. No matter how sore and tired we were mentally, physically, and emotionally, the best medicine was to keep our mouths shut and complain about nothing—or we probably wouldn't be around too long.

We were molded into the "property of the University of Minnesota athletic department." We soon found out that we had very little control of our lives. We were being trained and conditioned to be warriors, which meant that, when the governor of the State of Minnesota closed down all the state offices and universities because of deadly cold temperatures, the University of Minnesota football team had to press on and endure temperatures that dropped to fifty below zero, with a wind chill factor that made it feel far colder.

There was never ever any calling in sick. If we were sick, we had to show up at the football complex so team doctors and trainers could verify that we were not faking, and then make the necessary recommendations. If we got injured, we were up and back on the field in a matter of days.

We were being trained and conditioned to be able to withstand enormous amounts of physical, mental, and verbal ill-treatment. We were being trained and conditioned to be entertainers to crowds of hundreds of thousands of screaming fans, all cheering us to victory—or defeat. We were being trained and conditioned to never show signs of pain. We rarely cried, and usually didn't talk about our feelings, either. The only acceptable emotions came with preparing for a football game—the emotions of rage and excitement. It became difficult to decipher when players were really in need of medical attention or whether they were being "cream puffs" or "wusses" about an injury. Our entire lives were impacted by the training and conditioning that we went through.

In the book, The Mis-Education of the Negro, the father of black history, Dr. Carter Godwin Woodson, once had this to say about control and training: "When you control a man's thinking you do not have to worry about his actions. You do not have to tell him not to stand here or go yonder. He will find his 'proper place' and will stay in it. You do not need to send him to the back door. He will go without being told. In fact, if there is no back door, he will cut one for his special benefit."

We were under what I would call the "mis-education of the athlete." We were definitely trained and conditioned to know our "proper place." We never questioned why it was that we went out and entertained on the football field each weekend, bringing in millions and millions of dollars to the athletic program and the university—dollars that we never saw. We never questioned why our coaches were bringing home six-figure salaries and we were living on a fixed income and had to report every penny given to us. We never questioned why it was that we lived in small dorm rooms or apartments while our coaches and their families lived in three- and four-hundred-thousand-dollar homes, and, in some cases, received even more benefits. We never questioned why we had to walk, ask other people for rides, or ride bikes to get to where we needed to go while our coaches had multiple brand new vehicles for themselves and their families. We learned to do as they said and not as they did; we learned to live as they said and not as they lived. We were trained to never question these things, and so life went on.

With the start of school and football season came more responsibility. We had to carry the demands of a full class schedule in addition to the demands that already existed with football. But the thing that preoccupied and amazed me the most were the words spoken by "Big Mike" over the summer. He had told us that the beginning of the season and school would open the floodgates to more females. And he was right. It was intoxicating. After every game, hundreds of females would stand weathering the cold temperatures outside the Metro Dome—win or lose—waiting to connect with one or more of the players. In nearly every class, there was always one female lurking for her golden opportunity to meet me because of my "football player" title. In our dorms, which we shared with regular students, females would place their names on the long waiting list just to be housed in our dorms, hoping for bragging rights to say they lived with and knew players on the team. As crazy as it may sound, even guys yearned for those same bragging rights. At the stores, walking through the campus, in the nightclubs, at the malls, or anywhere else women could be found, the opportunities to build a mightier, stronger team of females were always present. The moment they caught wind that we played for the University of Minnesota's football team, it was on. The words "football player" did all the talking for us. And the females came in all colors, shapes, and sizes, from various locations throughout the state and country. I had never seen anything like it before, and even the brief introduction to the life of college athletics during my recruitment trips couldn't compare to the real thing.

Whenever we traveled to parties and other social events around town, there would always be anywhere from fifteen to seventy of us, depending upon the event. We did everything together. Outside of the classroom, our college experience was much different than that of the regular college students.

Our dinners came at different times, giving us the opportunity to be filled with foods like steaks and pork chops on a regular basis. In addition, we were served a catered meal once a week. We had our own tutors and advisors. We had our own computer labs and workout facilities. We had our own doctors who took care of us when we were sick or injured. We had our own airplane that took us to away games. We traveled without ever having to set foot inside most airports; we were escorted over the runways by police or highway patrol. We stayed in the finest hotels in the cities we traveled to for games. *This is the life!*

Nicknames were also quite popular within the team. Nearly everyone had one, and it was unusual to call someone by their first name. We had: T-Rock, Scubbie, Duce-Duce, Cheese Cake, Tim Dog, J-Wood, Crawdad, T-Well, Big Dean, D-White, Fat Cat, Crazy Cross, Ruf-Ruf, Smoke, Lemon

Lime, Big Cobe, J-Bird, T-Bird, Big Biscuit, Hi-T, Scooter, Hamma Time, Sea Food, Greyhound, G-Nut, Big Booty, Jimmy Jam, SJ, Fish, Sweet Lou, O, OG, B. G., Rodney O, D-Harv, Big Bal, K-Rock, Big B, Money Mike, Dark Side, Popcorn, Pick-A-Lo, Twig, Scooter, Wet-Foot, Mo-Jo, V-Hip, Dump Truck, L-L, Rodeo, and Tumble Weed—just to name a few.

My nicknames ranged from T-Wat to Two-Step, my old nickname given to me by Grandma Mae during my childhood. This type of closeness was what it took to survive in the profession of student-athlete.

With this closeness also came conflict. Big D, another freshman in my class, weighed in at over 300 pounds and bench-pressed over 400 pounds coming out of high school. Numbers like this gave him the chance to be the bully over most of our freshman class.

"What you call me, a punk?" he barked one day in the freshman locker room to another player who had said nothing.

"No, no man, umm … I … I … didn't say nothing," Little Ken frighteningly responded.

And with my attitude of "me against the world," topped by the fact that I wasn't going to let anyone bully me, it was just a matter of time before the two of us clashed and bumped heads.

That day would come while I was working out before a game with a freshman who'd had to "red-shirt." If you were "red shirted," you didn't play in games during your first year, which gave us an additional year to develop physically and mentally for college football.

I knew this day had been coming for a while. For many weeks, Big D had been sizing me up during our conversations—our most recent regular conversations had been ending with my teammates trying to detain him. "What's up, then, you want some of this T-Wat?" was the end of many conversations. I would casually walk away, trying to avoid a confrontation. But, on this day, word had spread that one female that Big D had been trying to win over since setting foot on campus had expressed interested in meeting me. This gave Big D the window of opportunity he had been waiting for.

"Yeah, I'm going to beat yo' ass when we get back upstairs, T-Watt," he continuously said, walking back and forth during our hour-and-a-half weight-lifting session. "You just wait until you come upstairs," he said as he headed for the stairs to the locker room.

"Man, T-Wat, what you going to do?" several of my freshman teammates asked.

"I'm going to handle that punk," I said flexing into the mirror.

I had played it over and over in my mind a thousand times how my punches probably wouldn't do much to his 300-pound, pretty-much-fat-free frame. In my search for what to do, I came across a huge pole lying on the weight room floor. That pole was now going to become my weapon of defense. Just as before, I played the confrontation over and over in my mind a thousand times. *Now, if I hit him in the head with this pole, I'm probably going to kill him or send him to the hospital.* I was the last person to leave the weight room.

When I arrived and opened the door to the locker room, Big D was standing with his back toward me; he was getting ready to put his pants on. Perfect, I thought to myself, not breaking a stride to get to him before he turned around. "What's up now?" I yelled out just before I landed the pole on his right shoulder and then again to his body before I took off out of the locker room and headed outside where I could escape from being grabbed by this mountain of a man who had not even been dazed by my blows with the pole.

Before I knew it, the two of us were sitting before our head coach being reprimanded for our actions. Well, mainly I was being reprimanded because I had been the only one who had landed blows. "Both of you were wrong in this matter. However, Tommy, your action of using a weapon could have resulted in being kicked off the team. Any further actions like this by you will result in you packing your bags and heading back home." This was the stern warning that came from Coach Wacker. He didn't have to say anymore.

From that day to the present, Big D and I have carried a mutual respect for each other, bringing an end to that cycle of confrontation. I had to learn to survive free of violence in my new world, or I wasn't going to last.

Players on the team whose families could not afford to send money for the basics of life at college were able to apply for additional funds through the Pell Grant. That's how I came to be sitting in Ms. Dallas's office, trying to figure out how I could let her know that I qualified for the student aide without telling her all my business.

"So, how much money do your parents make?" she calmly asked.

"I don't know."

"Well, what do they do for a living?" She was preparing to jump on the Internet to search for the average income for their jobs.

"I don't know," I said, gripping the arms of the chair in frustration.

"Well, you do live with your parents, don't you?"

"No, I don't live with my parents or my grandparents," I snapped back.

"Okay, I got it. You must either be married or a ward of the court, which means you can file independently," she said, pulling out a new set of forms.

"Don't bother." I motioned for her to put the forms back in the drawer. "Neither of those applies to me."

"If that's the case, who has custody over you back in Denver?" She leaned forward in her chair.

"No one."

"No one?" she retorted. "How can that be?"

"No one," I said again.

"Hum ... what about insurance? Do you have any?"

*What ... insurance?* The only thing I knew about insurance was going to Denver General Hospital, which was considered by many to be the poor man's hospital—you got whatever you needed fixed and they sent you a bill in the mail, which you ripped up and threw in the trash—fool-proof insurance at its cheapest.

"No, I don't have any insurance." I sighed.

"Tommy, there's nothing I can do for you if you don't tell me your situation. Everything that is said in this room stays in this room," she finally said. She gave me a look that said my secret was safe with her. With that reassurance, I released my story in a flood, leaving her, as she said, flabbergasted. "Wow. Tommy, in all my many years of being here at the University of Minnesota, we have never had a situation like yours come through our doors before. But. I'll tell you what. I am going to see to it that we do everything we can to get you a petition to file independent."

The process following this meeting was long and tedious. I had to get letters confirming my situation from the few people back home in Denver who knew some of the details. The end result showed me that she, Ms. Dallas, was a woman of her word—she did not let anything I had said go beyond the few coaches on the staff who also needed to write letters of support for me. Her efforts even landed me an opportunity to receive money beyond the Pell Grant funds for coats and boots each year to help me survive the freezing cold winters in Minnesota. Thanks, Ms. Dallas.

Making it through my first quarter of college was tough. It was tough and humbling adjusting to a new level of sports at the Division I level and seeing several of my teammates quit and give up their scholarships and go back home. My performance in the classroom suffered—when I wasn't "chasing skirts" and missing classes, I was focusing solely on football, hoping to get my big break so I could go on to the NFL.

I had naively convinced myself that my new-found behavior of dating lots and lots of females would only be short term until I made it back home to my girlfriend. And, with each day, I became more and more blindly submerged into a lifestyle that victimizes many men who over indulge with females to cover up deeply embedded self-esteem problems.

Even though I had suspected that I wasn't doing too well in school, I didn't understand how badly I was doing until it was time to meet with my tutor in preparation for my final exams and I couldn't tell her one thing that I had remembered learning in my classes. During our brief session, she sat looking at me, shaking her head in disgust. "Tommy, this is not a good thing.

You are smarter than this. What are you going to do with your life if you don't graduate from college?"

What! Graduate? I'm going to the NFL, I thought to myself. In her eyes I was just another athlete suffering from the "dumb-jock" syndrome. To some degree, she was right. In my case, I was very capable of doing the work, but school had not been my focus. That quarter I received my first F, flunking my math class, a subject that I had always been very strong in. I still was not totally convinced that the world of college academics was for me.

The heavy burden of trying to find a place to stay in Denver would be one that I would have to carry with me constantly each time I left Minnesota to return home for breaks and vacations. Fortunately, this time I would make plans to stay with Ozzie. Now I was ready to head home.

As I planned to return to Denver for Christmas break, I was elated with the anticipation of seeing my newborn son—just three months old—and my girlfriend. Walking through the door and seeing my son Martice was one of the greatest moments of my life. I wanted him to remain in my arms forever. I finally had the opportunity to love as I had never had before. It was my goal to show Martice every ounce of unconditional love that existed in me.

It was also during this visit home that I started to feel the strain of living the life I was living chasing females in Minnesota and having a girlfriend back home who knew nothing about it. My mind was being yanked back and forth between the two worlds—one world calling me to do the right thing and be a responsible father and, possibly, a husband. This was a world that was full of love, but I found it confusing, because love for me when I was growing up had always come with a price—a price that left me feeling alone and abandoned, and in lots of deep, hidden pain.

The other world back in Minnesota offered—supposedly—"no-strings-attached" physical and financial relationships with females who didn't know anything about me, which lessened my chances of getting hurt.

Over the next year or so, I would eventually push my girlfriend away from me, gravitating more toward the relationships in Minnesota, which allowed me to be protected and unexposed behind the masks of being a "ladies man" and "athlete." These are two masks that many men adopt to hide their insecurities from the world. As time went on, I also discovered that both men and women alike go through life hiding their insecurities behind the masks of money, fame, education, occupations, possessions, drugs, fraternities and sororities, gangs, titles, and social status—to name just a few.

The fact that my girlfriend had to put her life on hold to take care of our son, whom we had both taken part in making, was a thorn in my side that

I had to carry with me for some time, causing me to constantly feel guilty about my decision to leave Colorado.

My holiday stay in Colorado was both elating and frightening. It was great to look into the eyes of my son and become mesmerized with the love that comes with the creation of someone special. At the same time, visiting Martin and Mom in prison, where they lived under the complete domination of other human beings, brought back many painful memories of when I first visited Mom in prison as a little kid. Though they were incarcerated in different places, their lives were controlled by the same system. And, if that pain was not enough, seeing Grandma Louise in the nursing home never for one moment taking her eyes off the ceiling, and never comprehending that her grandson, who owed her everything, was sitting next to her, brought me to tears. In the early stages of my childhood, I had always equated being an adult with freedom, but the reality of having Mom, Dad, Grandma Louise, and Martin physically limited to facilities, and seeing Levi and Melony being psychologically limited to Five Points, contradicted those childhood ideas and beliefs. This total re-submersion into the past I had left months earlier made my trip back to college bittersweet. I felt I was leaving a part of me behind—Martice—but life had to go on.

With a year having passed since I had attended the Martin Luther King march in Denver, I was now standing in sub-zero temperatures at the capitol building in downtown St. Paul in honor of another MLK Day. And, what a disappointing sight it was.

"Where are all the black people at?" I asked my lady friend who had brought me to the event.

"Normally we don't come out to *stuff like this,*" she responded.

*Stuff like this?* I said to myself. *Don't they know this event is all about them?* Just days earlier I had been the one player who stood up to our coaching staff with very little support from others on the team to have our workout on MLK Day canceled. Despite being granted the day off, many of the black players on the team still decided to work out. *What was up with this? Maybe it's just Minnesota.* Regardless of the cause of the nonchalant attitudes of blacks in the state, my days of standing up for the rights of others who did not seem interested in standing up for themselves were over. *It's all about me.*

Despite my focus, for the remainder of the year I continued to struggle in the classroom and struggle to adjust to the very demanding life of the collegiate athlete. I was doing the bare minimum of work just to stay eligible for football. I was introduced to, but did not fully understand, the concept that football and the classroom worked hand in hand; the more I missed class, the more extra running I had to do. I started off many of my mornings extra early, having to do a thousand yards of up-downs with a couple other players who also did not get the concept of going to class.

"Up, down, up, down," my position coach howled during the drill that typically took forty-five minutes to complete, giving us fifteen minutes to rest and gather our thoughts before we had to run again with the rest of the team at 6:30. One thing that I learned to do during this time was to measure my sleep throughout the night when I knew we had to get up and run in the morning. Waking up throughout the night, I'd glance over at the clock and compute how much more time I had to sleep. This kept my mind set on the morning run so it wouldn't take me by surprise.

Throwing up and falling out was pretty common for me and several others on the team. By far I was the worst. My lack of confidence in myself to make it through many workouts, in addition to my resistance to being shouted at by the coaches, made for many long workouts.

"Run your ass through the line, Watson," constantly rained from their mouths.

I had assumed that off-season running would be early morning jogs followed by a little weight lifting—all done within an hour. I was mistaken. Our entire 6:30 am run itself lasted an hour. It was all sprinting, everything was timed, and, if one player from our hundred-plus-member team didn't make his time during a sprint, that particular sprint did not count for anyone.

"Come on, Tommy, run through the damn line," my teammates shouted as I stood bent over with my hands on my knees, dying from exhaustion. Bending over during a sprint to catch your breath was a sign of weakness, we were told by our strength coach, so doing it usually caused us to be assigned more running. Needless to say, between the extra running with the team and the individual punitive running, I was in pretty good shape.

# Chapter VIII

## *This Pain I am Feeling—Part 2*

Over ninety thousand yelling voices and stomping pairs of feet threatened to bring down the house as the University of Minnesota prepared to play the Penn State Nittany Lions in a historic game. This was to be Penn State's first-ever Big Ten game since they had become a part of the conference earlier in this new season of college football—a season in which I had improved my performance and was now given the chance to travel with the team to the away games.

"I was there" flags were everywhere—on fans' heads, in their hands, and on their cars—as our three-bus caravan, surrounded by the state patrol, sped past mile-long traffic jams. It seemed that everyone was en route for the stadium. Some fans gave us the finger, some mooned us, and others gave us a welcoming cheer as our buses finally pulled into the stadium parking lot full of tailgaters, drinkers, and onlookers, all anxiously awaiting the highly anticipated game. Television news trucks with huge satellite dishes lined up around the entrance into the stadium. Every reporter was yearning to catch an interview from key players on the team. Young, enthusiastic fans lined up solidly behind the lengthy barricades, hoping to get autographs. Stadium security people and staff looked on in awe as our mammoth team passed through, while hundreds of hecklers yelled from the balconies above. "Today is the day, ya'll go down," seemed to be the mutual theme coming from the crazed hoards.

Inside the locker room, we could hear the pounding footsteps of over ninety thousand fans over our heads. Their impact caused the helmets in the lockers to vibrate against the metal cages. And, every once in a while, an occasional "Minnesota sucks!" came shooting through the slightly cracked window high on the wall of the locker room. The faces of my teammates remained stern and emotionless—the perfect "game-time" face. Everyone quietly engaged in his own pre-game ritual: throwing up, using the bathroom, picking his nose, napping, eating, pacing back and forth, reading, watching television, praying, and—the most preferred—listening to blaring music, fortunately through personal earpieces. Whatever one had to do to get ready, it was okay, because it was almost time to play. Butterflies creamed my stomach in anticipation of the show about to take place. Everyone had to find the groove that was right for him to ease the volcanic pre-game jitters that came with playing huge games against noble Big Ten Conference opponents and before crowds of thirty thousand to one hundred thousand crazed fans. There were lots of perspiring palms during our final team prayer. Then it was time to head down to the field.

It was "game time." Time to strap it on. The long walk down the cemented tunnel created echoes—an army of clogging cleats—as we approached for battle. On both sides of the tunnel wall stood paramedics, cheerleaders, reporters, security personnel, and prospective high school recruits—all tense in anticipation, along with everyone else, of the big game. The final descent onto the field provoked thousands of enthusiastic "boo's," which sparked excitement in each of us. With the roars from the crowd, we couldn't even hear the player next to us, who might be trying to wish us good luck! As soon as our last players arrived on the field, there came another roar—the roar of a vicious lion—over the stadium speakers. It was now the Nittany Lions' turn to enter onto the field. And, if there was anyone in the state of Pennsylvania not listening to the game on the radio or watching it on TV, even they could have heard the erupting crowd of wild and crazy fans as they showed their love for the home team.

The hot and humid Pennsylvania air engulfed every square inch of the beautifully cut grass, giving it a silky look as the sun directed its powerful rays down on its green surface.

The smell of hot dogs and fresh popcorn streamed across the field as we took our positions on the field for kickoff. Tiers of fans were stacked on each other like building blocks, leaving no sign of an empty seat. Blaring through the speakers was Madonna's smash hit, "Holiday." The music rocked through my ears, causing me to momentarily bob my head to the beat, in final preparation.

Instantly, I was transported back for a moment to the many times I had watched Penn State play in this very same stadium on television as a teen. What an honor to now be able to get an inside view of all of this drama as it unfolded right before my eyes; the thought that I was taking part in the very game that many others were watching at home, wishing to be in, filled my stomach with more untamed butterflies.

Finally, play began. The game went back and forth, with both teams delivering big hit after big hit. The scoreboard lit up from one side to the other as both of our teams scored touchdown after touchdown. Blood and snot flew from the helmets of many of the players. Bones cracked and jerseys ripped during monstrous tackles.

The feeling of defeat that we were hoping to put on the Nittany Lions, in our party to welcome them into the Big Ten Conference, was, by the end of the hard-fought, three-hour game, a feeling that we had to carry home with us. Our exit from the field was followed by the chant from the capacity crowd, "Nah nah, nah nah nah nah, hey hey-aay, good-bye." In addition to that, hearing the song, "Another One Bites The Dust," blaring from the stadium speakers and echoing through our locker room only drew more tears from many players on our team who were already sobbing.

The following week, it was on to San Diego to play against future NFL superstars Marshall Faulk, Darney Scoot, and their comrades from the San Diego State University. For many of us on the team, it was our first-time-ever to visit California. The beautiful ocean beach on which our hotel sat seemed like heaven on earth. From the balcony of my room, we could see huge naval ships coming and going through the sea haze in the distance. My roommate and I sat mesmerized by this sight for hours. Big, strong palms grew alongside almost every street, providing sporadic spots of shade over the sidewalks and giving pedestrians just enough relief from the heat.

We usually arrived in town a day before our game. In San Diego we had spent part of our free time during the day hanging out at the local mall, where many of us had had the opportunity to meet many intrigued females. Jokingly we told them that we were having a pool party at our hotel later on that night. We really didn't believe we would ever see any of them again once our paths separated at the mall. To our surprise, many of the females took this to be true. They told their friends who told more friends, and, by the end of the night, our hotel was being bombarded by waves of females dressed in their "Daisy Duke" shorts, mini-skirts, and halter tops—all hoping to hang out with the team. With this taking place well after our 10:30 curfew, all we could do was sit and look from our windows as security guards and coaches spent a good portion of the night turning the crowds away.

"Man, can you believe them females really showed up like that last night?" I whispered to one of my teammates at our morning breakfast.

"Yeah, T, that just goes to show that we are in demand across the nation. These females all want a piece of an athlete, only to be left in the end with a broken heart," Earl, my veteran teammate, said, obviously used to this type of thing.

He was exactly right. It was amazing how many women were willing to sell their souls and totally disregard certain levels of self-respect just to hang out with people they perceived to be special. And most often they were truly left broken-hearted from their unrealistic expectations. Each one hoped she would be the one woman who could come along and change one of us so she could become his "one and only." On the surface, it appeared that many of us athletes didn't have to worry about experiencing a broken heart because there were always at least four women to replace that one who got away for whatever reason. But many of us did what we did because of broken hearts and disappointments at the hands of women we'd known in previous relationships. In my case, my broken heart had come from parental neglect.

I would later discover that this lifestyle also takes a toll on many athletes and entertainers, making it very difficult for them to experience "true love" when they have a chance. Often we couldn't tell whether a woman was interested in us as an individual or as an athlete, and that only added to that hidden void of insecurity. As a result, many of these men ended up living very isolated lives later on, whether they were married or single.

Nevertheless, by the end of the game, we were leaving the field once again to that infamous chant of defeat from the crowd, "Nah nah, nah nah nah nah, hey hey-aay, good-bye."

This chant set the tone and became the standard for the rest of our season as we finished with a 2-9 record. My duties on the field had been, for the most part, limited to special teams.

By spring of my second year of college, there was a quiet storm on the horizon. To many of the people around me, I appeared to be a gracious gigolo and tough guy, but on the inside I was falling apart. Everything I had been running from—all the pain and hurt from the past—was starting to catch up with me. Behind closed doors, I was falling into a state of depression, spending many nights crying from hurt, as I had as a child. Massive headaches rang through my head constantly. Many times, as I walked across the towering Washington Avenue Bridge, which stood nearly 200 feet above the raging waters of the Mississippi River, thoughts filled my mind about ending the many years of pain—just ending it all. Day after day, my mind was in a constant war with my battered emotions. Go ahead, jump and everything will be all right. You won't have to ever deal with this pain anymore. The storm that had been brewing inside of me for many years was finally starting to erupt. Each time the thought of suicide came upon me, it was immediately followed by the words of one of my high school teachers who often said to our class, "Suicide is a permanent solution to a temporary problem." But my problems seemed more than temporary; they had lasted almost my entire life.

My grades had fallen to a point where my scholarship was now in jeopardy. "Tommy, this is your last warning. Either pull your grades up by the end of the summer or you are gone," were the words that came from university's athletic director at the end of our meeting in his office.

Day after day after day, I tried to continue with the normal routines that wouldn't expose the "inner me." "Man, I am cool as a fan," I responded to one of my curious teammates one day, who sensed something different about me—words of a fool in need of help, not knowing how to ask for it. At times, my headaches became so intense that my vision became skewed, turning the sights before me to a blur. My eyes filled with tears from the pain of this internal battle that raged inside me. Nighttime was even more frightening, as I always had to face him—that wounded child who had never stopped crying from childhood. I hadn't realized it, but he had been lurking within me since those difficult days. I was like an injured soldier stumbling through a smoke-filled battlefield, trying to avoid enemy bombs raining from the sky, searching across a sea of dead bodies, hoping to find one trustworthy face for help and a pathway out of all the madness. My life was spiraling out of control.

Finally one day after a meeting with my academic advisor, Ms. Benson, my efforts to keep everything together came to an end. She watched from a distant corner as my body surrendered to all the pressure and pain. My head dropped, crashing down on the books that lay open on the table before me. I couldn't take it anymore. The tears flowed as freely in public as they had when I was a child.

"Tommy, are you okay?"

I struggled to gather myself, to act as though nothing were wrong.

"Something told me to follow you in here after our meeting," she said, closing the door in our team lounge. And with that, the tears reassembled themselves in my eyes. There was no more running from myself; there was nowhere to hide. I was now wearing the face of the little hurting child from the past, a face that was no longer a distant foreigner. "Tommy, we have to get you some help."

I was in an ocean of pain, not knowing who to trust or even how to trust. Why in the hell couldn't Mom and Dad have been better parents for me and my siblings? Having no answer before me, I could do nothing but weep and weep in the arms of a concerned Ms. Benson. There was no manual or handbook for a person in my shoes experiencing a rock-bottom war with the past.

For the first time, someone had seen me display emotions of pain and defeat in a public setting. I couldn't believe it. Ms. Benson and our lead academic advisor Brian offered me the opportunity for counseling, but, even after falling to an all-time low in life, I couldn't avail myself of the opportunity. My pride would not allow me to see a shrink.

"Tommy, are you sure you don't want to see Dr. Jones? He does good work, and everything you say will be between the two of you."

"No, really, I'm okay," I said leaving her office after what seemed like hours of trying to pull myself back together.

On top of all this, I had received word from back home that Grandma Louise was nearing death. The last stages of Alzheimer's had taken its toll on her. *When are all the drama and problems going to cease?*

Despite all the negative things I was feeling in Minnesota, I knew things would be far worse for me if I were kicked out of school and sent back to Denver, which was the garden of all my pain. With this fear in mind, I had to find it within myself to work through the obstacles and remain in Minnesota. *I have to do this for my own good.*

By the end of the summer quarter, having taken a boatload of additional classes to retain my scholarship, I finished my academic probation period off with the highest grade point average I ever achieved in college, 2.8.

The lack of discipline I had shown during the previous winter and spring workouts would have made it even easier for the school to take my scholarship from me. This, too, would be an area in which I needed to improve. Enduring our grueling morning workouts, I made it my personal mission each day to get better. And that I did. By the end of that spring, the headlines of the *Star Tribune* newspaper read, "Watson blossoms in the spring," signifying the improvement I had made during our spring practice—supposedly the avenue to more playing time in the big games.

Despite the great effort I had put forth to retain my scholarship, I was still facing my feelings of pain and fear; I had only learned how to shut my eyes a little tighter at night as I tried not to conjure up the "boogie man" of the past. After Grandma Louise's death in the middle of football season, I had come to that crossroad again, but this time it was different. Grandma Louise was no more, it was out of my control. There was no more resting on the hope that somehow the Alzheimer's in her body would reverse itself and bring back the Grandma Louise from my childhood. This was something final.

But, unlike the last time I had fallen into a state of depression, this time I did not have to spend so much time alone. Now that football season had started back up in my third year, I found myself rooming with the same player—known as "CD"—at the hotel each night before our away games. This allowed me a chance to eventually express some of the thoughts that roamed in my mind back in my solo room at the dorm. As I entered my third year of college, that was exactly what I needed.

Before this year, I had been playing the game of football literally to hurt people—choking, punching, and kicking my opponents. On one occasion, we were going up the tunnel into the locker room at halftime in a game we were losing to the University of Wisconsin when, out of the blue, I heard a voice behind me calling, "Watson. Hey, Watson!" I stopped and turned around to see who was calling me. "Hey, bud, you don't have to do me like that," one of the Wisconsin players contested. "We're home boys. I'm from Colorado too."

"Are you from Five Points?" I asked, already knowing the answer.

"No, I'm from Fort Collins."

"Well, you're not from Five Points, so I got to do you like that," I said, walking away. I had so much anger inside that I couldn't even get his point that my behavior on the football field had gone way beyond the rules of the game. My life and all of my emotions were trapped in a bottle and seeking an outlet.

That outlet came when I began to sit and talk with my teammate CD into the early hours of the morning before games. Many of our talks initially centered around typical things that guys talk about—nothing that had any real substance. Week after week our conversations grew to include more serious stuff about the neighborhoods where we had grown up, and our families. His neighborhood in Houston, Texas, had a lot in common with my neighborhood back home in Denver. We had both faced similar problems— the same problems faced in most inner city neighborhoods: drugs, poverty, and violence. The thing that separated our two lives was our family situations. And I was shocked that he did not judge me when I started to open up to him and tell him a little bit about my life growing up back home in Denver.

"Man, how did it make you feel going through that?" he would always ask at the end of my stories.

"I don't really know," was my response each time. "I don't know." And I would break into tears.

"Man, it looks like you still dealing with a lot of pain from your past," he said one night during one of our conversations. "I had a similar type of pain when I lost my favorite cousin. He died right in front of me—shot at a nightclub back home. That incident made me turn to the healer of all pain—God."

Now, I had always believed in God, but I just didn't believe he was watching over me—not with all the hardship that I had had to face. I was not even going to go there in that conversation with CD. And so I turned over and went to sleep. Where was God when I was going through all that stuff?

Despite our differences of opinion on this matter, we continued our relationship of sharing our pasts with each other for the remainder of the football season. It was wonderful to relieve myself of some of the heavy burdens of the past. Our conversations were a form of therapy. Talking about this stuff was something I had never done before. It felt great.

And, by the end of the season, we finished with another losing record and no explanation for my lack of playing time, despite my much-improved spring performance.

In my third year of school, due to my lack of playing time, it was obvious that my journey to the NFL was going to take a little longer than I had planned,. Knowing this, I had to buy myself more time in college, which meant declaring a major.

Early in my college career, I had bounced around between business management and African American studies. My choice for business management had only to do with the fact that many people said it paid well, and it sounded good when someone asked me what my major was. My choice of African American studies had to do with the fact that I was African American and I knew "everything" about African Americans. It was a major that I thought would surely keep me eligible for football. I would later learn that being African American no more guaranteed me the right to all knowledge about African Americans than it did for anyone who was not African American—a humbling revelation, but one that I needed to learn.

During this time, I had also enrolled in a class on the civil rights movement, in which I felt sure I'd get a passing grade and stay eligible for football. My knowledge on this subject was very limited. The only thing I knew about the movement was that Dr. Martin Luther King, Jr., had played a big part in it, and, of course, I had attended many modern-day marches.

I had heard a couple of stories from Dad about growing up in Little Rock, Arkansas, and how, during these times, he and his siblings had to walk something like ten miles to school with white people chasing them and throwing rocks at them.

"Ya'll kids today don't know what hard is. When me and my sisters and brothers were you all's age, we had to walk ten miles to school while being hit with rocks when we passed through white neighborhoods," he told us. It seemed as if, every time Dad told that story, both the miles and the obstacles they had to face became greater.

"Y'all kids today don't know what hard is. When me and my sisters and brothers were you all's age we had to walk twenty miles one way while being sprayed with water hoses, chased by dogs, spit on, and hit by rocks!"

Nevertheless, this was a movement that was distant to me. After all, I was of a younger generation and hadn't grown up in the South; so this movement was about as real for me as it was for any other little white kid who had grown up in an area with no link to the Movement. I felt no real connection to it. My expectations for getting anything out of this class, other than a passing grade, were extremely low.

"Man, what you doing taking a class on civil rights?" my close comrade Jake asked. "You ain't becoming one of those black power Negroes who sit around talking about slavery all day, are you?"

"Man, I needed something easy, and I needed to stay eligible. That's the only reason I'm taking this class," I assured him.

Neither of us had an inkling that, not only did this Movement benefit the two of us, it also benefited the lives of blacks and whites, men and women, heterosexuals and homosexuals, and many other groups throughout the world who searched for equality and liberation.

My farfetched statement about not being connected with the civil rights movement was about to be put to the test in a way that I had not anticipated. "Good morning, class. I am Mrs. Walker. Much of what you will be doing in this class will be writing essays based upon what you observe. Much of your writing will focus on a series of tapes we'll be watching each class period called Eyes on the Prize. I was pleased. Sounds pretty easy to me. If there's one thing I'm good at, it's watching movies. "So come prepared to take notes during our next class."

The following Thursday, I returned for the second class in time to jump into the series, Eyes On the Prize, which I had never heard of. I thought it sounded interesting. With the tape in progress, it didn't take long for me to discover that the title of the series was actually the theme song: "I know the one thing I did right was the day I started to fight ..."

Images of the movement flashed across the screen during the preview—images of angry, white police officers beating blacks with their nightsticks as they sat in silence at food counters. Images of angry, white mobs with guns, rocks, bottles, sticks, and chains surrounding schools and school buses where black children sat in fear. Images of black men, women, and kids being sprayed with high-pressure fire hoses that shredded the bark from trees as it scoured over hurt and injured bodies lying cradled on the ground. Images of the body of a black man hanging lifeless from a tree with a rope around his neck, while crowds of whites cheered and celebrated beneath his dead carcass. Images of crosses burning on the front lawns of black families. Images of the bloody faces of women and kids who had been kicked, punched, spat upon, and then thrown into the back of police wagons while being nearly chewed to pieces by vicious police dogs. And then we watched footage of a crowd of nearly ten thousand people in Duluth, Minnesota, who had turned out to witness and celebrate the hanging of three black men. *What in the hell kind of movie is this?*

Finally, I couldn't take it anymore. I was appalled. I grabbed my bag and stormed out of the classroom, vowing not to return. I burned with anger. *How in the hell can a black professor show stuff like that to anyone? And how in the hell can white people be that damn cruel to any human being, and then say that black people act like animals and shouldn't be mad about the past?* I couldn't believe what I had witnessed. I continued to storm down the stairs trying to avoid eye contact with every white face that passed me in an effort to prevent myself from unleashing my wrath on one of them for no reason other than what I had just witnessed during my first exposure to Eyes On the Prize. It had been such a painful reality.

As I walked back to the dorm after deciding that I wasn't going to ride the bus—which was a big decision since the University of Minnesota is one of the biggest campuses in the country—I came across my buddy Gus. Gus was an older African American gentleman who had been launched into homelessness after falling down on his luck when he came to Minnesota to go to college many years ago. He had dirty clothes, ash-colored skin, foul odor, and rotten teeth. He hadn't combed his wooly hair in years, and it looked as if rats had been playing in it. It was easy for most people to keep on walking when he approached them with his cup in the middle of campus, asking for spare change. But, for me, there was always a looming feeling of connection and compassion that ran through my veins for him and others in hardship situations. This allowed me to discover the great wisdom that Gus possessed. I was amazed how someone who was homeless could be up to date on all the world's current events.

I sat beside him on the bench, surrounded by pigeons, all fighting for the crumbs Gus threw to them from his sandwich. My lips were still poked out in fury. What I wanted to know from Gus was what he thought about the whole black-and-white thing in America—and racism. "Gus, what is your take on the relationship of blacks and whites in our country?"

Gus started off with a question to ponder before he gave me his spiel on this matter. "Well, Young Blood," as he always called me, "let me ask you this. Do you think America's somewhat changed attitude towards blacks today has to do more with issues of morality or money?"

"Uhm, uhm … I don't know." I wondered where he was going with this question.

"You see, Young Blood, black people spend between $400-500 billion dollars a year in the American economy. We lose over $200 billion dollars a year due to unjust wage discrimination. Today, we are still fighting the same fight for affirmative action that we have been fighting for decades. You see, affirmative action ain't no bad thing, but the problem with it is, too many groups who don't share the same past and struggles with the blacks are being thrown in the same pot to fight for one cause. Gays, white women, people with disabilities—all are coming to the table with different pasts and struggles, which require different strategies and solutions. We need to be able to support these other groups in their causes, but do so using a separate agenda. Take cancer for instance. Each type of cancer organization focuses on and raises money for a specific type of cancer. They are all still working toward the same overall goal, which is to cure cancer; however, each is in pursuit of the goal from a different angle. We got to be more domestically independent as black people and be aware of the strategies that have been put in place to keep us from reaching liberation.

"You see, Young Blood, there was a time many decades ago when a high proportion of blacks were going to college, even in those times and with those challenges. But, as soon as the doors opened up for blacks to be able to come to white institutions like this one, our mission became more focused on being one of that handful of blacks to be allowed into these white colleges. As a result of this, our black colleges suffered, and we have more black men in jail today than we do on college campuses.

"Young Blood, when I was younger, the Negro Baseball League was the best thing going since cotton candy, and the entire country knew that. Blacks had played in the National Baseball League before Jackie Robinson. Jackie Robinson was the first one they allowed back in the National Baseball League. That broke the color barrier and left the Negro League colorless. The Negro League eventually closed shop because all the up-and-coming black baseball stars were trying to get to the National Baseball League.

"So, Young Blood, there it is in a nutshell. We have been hoodwinked—both blacks and whites—and that is why the rich continues to get richer and the poor continues to get poorer.

"This is exactly what affirmative action, the way it is today, does to our black communities. It takes our best away from our communities and leaves the rest of us to struggle to survive in these places that we call ghettos.

"You ask me what my take is about the black and white issues and racism in this country? My response is this: racism has never been about the color of your skin, or the color of anyone else's skin. Many of the things you young blacks face today on a day-to-day basis in our society that you may think is racism is not even close to it. Ignorance results from a lack of knowing someone or a lack of a relationship with someone. Ignorance causes individuals to call you racial names and follow you around in stores. Being ignorant doesn't make this type of thinking right. Racism is systemic and is about power, politics, and money. Racism is a powerful social idea that gives certain people access to opportunities and resources. So, really, what we are talking about is inequality, which impacts both whites and blacks. When Martin Luther King gathered folks in Washington DC in the 1960s, it wasn't about racism, it was about equality and justice for all Americans. Racism was one of the byproducts of the discriminatory behaviors. From the White House to our churches, all kinds of institutions have played a role in the way things are in this country today. That's why it's important for human beings to seek the truth for themselves and not ride on another person's understanding. And when one does that, he or she consumes "true" knowledge."

Wow. It would take years before I fully grasped many of the things Gus talked about. But, the most important thing I learned was that, in order to get knowledge, one had to go out and experience it, even if it meant experiencing it from presentations like Eyes on the Prize.

That conversation led me to go back to the civil rights class with a different attitude and a desire to learn a little something about my true history and about some of the "faces of courage" of that Movement—faces of people whose heads were bloody but unbowed. For the first time in my life, I was beginning to realize that every opportunity I had as a black person in this country was because men and woman, boys and girls, and blacks and whites had been hung from trees, beat by police, spit on, slapped, punched, kicked, raped, burned, bombed, drowned, rendered jobless, and shot for my right to be able to vote and sit in a class and play football and have access to an institution such as the University of Minnesota. By the end of the class, I had learned about Addie Mae Collins, Denise McNaire, Carole Robertson, and Cynthia Wesley who were killed in the bombing of a black church in Birmingham, Alabama, in 1963; Emmett Louis Till, a fourteen-year-old who was murdered for speaking to a white woman in Money, Mississipi, in

1955; and Medgar Evers, a civil rights leader who was killed by an assassin in Jackson, Mississippi, in 1963. And I learned more.

I discovered, after further study on my own, that this Movement involved people who had an enormous amount of education and who had great jobs, who were prominent entertainers and athletes. These people were different from many of today's high-profile athletes, entertainers, and public icons—male and female—who seem to be content with making an occasional financial donations because they don't want to get involved in the fight for equality, but would rather watch and benefit from a distance.

It did not seem to matter to many of these courageous fighters in the civil rights movement whether a person was a "have" or "have not." They were all in the fight together—from the Supreme Court to the basketball court.

I was a part of a generation that wanted everything here and now; we didn't care about tomorrow, and we didn't know anything about the past. Many of us gauged our happiness by the amount of money and "things" we could obtain.

This turned out to be the most important class that I ever took during my college career. I was able to leave the class feeling privileged, not only to be a black athlete, but also to be a black man and an American.

# Chapter IX

## *What If?*

I often found it tough to sit around and listen to how life was for many of my teammates back home and felt too embarrassed to share very much about the true world of Tommy Watson.

"Man, every time I go home, my family gives me a gift to welcome me back," someone once said. *What would it be like to return to a stable home and people who are thrilled about the fact that I came back from college? What would it be like if I didn't have to return to a neighborhood filled with violence?*

These moments were difficult for me because of my reality. I had to call ahead to find a place to stay during breaks and vacations, and I had to call people from the bus station in Denver to remind them that I was in town and needed to be picked up. It was also vital that I monitor the colors of my wardrobe to make sure they didn't violate the rules set up by the gangs in my neighborhood. Being that our colors at the University of Minnesota were maroon and gold, I had to be sure that the maroon clothing that was such a big part of my wardrobe could not be mistaken for red. Many times, returning home also meant facing heavy criticism from some of my family members for my lack of playing time; comments like, "Man, you done went all the way up to Minnesota to play ball and ain't even playing. I told you, you wasn't going to ever be nothing."

I often had deep feelings of guilt when I had to leave Denver to go back to college. The fact that I had to constantly ask other people for money, food, and shelter reinforced the comments that I would never amount to anything.

And, more and more, my dreams of making it to the NFL became less about me and more about showing the unbelievers in my family who cut me down at every chance.

Even though my hard work on the football field during spring ball the previous year didn't warrant me any more playing time during the regular season, I still decided that I was going to come back again and work twice as hard. I still had two more seasons ahead of me.

By the end of spring football, I had finished as MVP and had broken into the starting lineup at the running back position. Things were starting to look a bit promising for me. But we would have to still wait until the fall.

Darkness had finally settled over the city of Denver. There I was, during a brief break from school, rolling down the street driving Levi's decked-out minivan with the fancy rims and the booming sound system. Mom was with me. It felt good being back in Mom's presence. She was out of prison and had vowed to never go back to prison or jail again. She had made a new commitment to God while in prison—a commitment that she would start living a life only for him—no more shoplifting, using drugs, or selling drugs.

In the backseat sat Caroline, Levi's girlfriend. Caroline had always been nice to me; that's why I had offered to go and pick her up for Levi—in addition to the fact that I enjoyed driving his suave minivan.

Earlier in the day, my 1984 rusted Jetta had broken down. It had provided a great ride back to Colorado, and had just decided that the thin mountain air was too much; it needed a break.

Even though Mom was out of prison and doing better, I did not like staying at her house in Five Points because there was always too much activity going on in the four-complex apartments she lived in. The action was due to the fact that "Rough Rider," the leader of the notorious gang that Martin, Levi, and hundreds of other black males and females were a part of lived right next door to her. I can give Rough Rider and the rest of the gang members credit for only one thing—they all gave Mom ample respect, referring to her as "Mom" when they saw her. But at night bullets from AK-47s, sawed-off shotguns, nine millimeters, and Tec-9s whistled through the air, sometimes from enemy fire and other times just from gang members testing out their arsenal of weapons. Facing all of this, I made arrangements to spend my last couple of days with Uncle J.R., who was anxiously waiting for me at Mom's house so we could get back out to his quiet neighborhood in Montbello.

"Here comes the tricky part," I said to Mom and Caroline pulling up to the house. I had always had trouble trying to parallel park Levi's minivan, and this time was no different. Back and forth I went, trying to squeeze into the tight space between the two cars in front of Mom's house.

"Boy, do you want me to park the car?" Mom joked.

"Nah, I got it, don't you know I got skills?"

"Well yo' skills ain't working too well right now," Caroline yelled out from the back, throwing us all into laughter.

Back and forth I continued. And, as I struggled, I caught a glimpse of a suspicious-looking black Jeep Cherokee idling beneath the throbbing streetlight at the corner, which was about half a block away. Paying it not much mind, I continued my quest to park the mini-van.

"Man, I may need some divine intervention getting this thing parked."

"You're right about that," said Mom. We were all laughing. In the midst of our parking mayhem, we had no idea of what we were about to encounter.

At that very moment … *"Boom boom boom, pop pop pop"* filled the air. *What the hell …?* Now, I was pretty used to hearing gunshots in my neighborhood, but something in my head told me, *this time,* to get down because these shots sounded close. And, just like that, the windows on the van began to shatter. The unthinkable had occurred—this was a drive-by shooting, and we were the target. With my body hunched over, leaning toward the middle of the van, I covered my head and chest area with my arms and left knee, while my other foot somehow naturally rested on the brake, keeping the van from tearing off backwards into other cars. *"Boom boom boom, pop pop pop,"* the gunshots continued. The crashing and shattering of the glass continued inches above my head, and I started to prepare myself for the inevitable. Sparks from the shredded metal filled the inside of the minivan.

Everything around me seemed to slow down in that moment, and, before my eyes, I began to see flashing images from my life, as if this was the final glimpse for me. I saw quick images of those important faces around me—Mom, Martice, Melony, Martin, Carmen, Levi, Sherl, and Aunt Milly to name a few. Were these to be the last faces that I would see before leaving this world? I hadn't had a chance to say good-bye yet. Good-bye to Martice, good-bye to Mom, good-bye to my sisters, brothers, and friends. Was this the way life was going to end for me? I hadn't had a chance to say I'm sorry to all of those I had wronged. I hadn't even had the chance to ask God to forgive me for all the sins I had committed. As the shots continued ringing into the vehicle, I prepared myself for death. *Good-bye world.* I simply closed my eyes and waited for the bullets to pierce my body and soul. The shooting continued.

After what seemed like an eternity, suddenly, just as the gunshots had started, they stopped. And, in that instant, there was the most frightening sound of silence that I had ever heard in my life. My eyes were still tightly closed, and I allowed them to open only for a quick peek. I touched my face and check to see if I had really survived such a moment. When I realized I had survived, I also realized I had survived with no injuries. *Amazing! Thank you, Jesus!*

Seeing that I was okay in the midst of all the silence, and not knowing whether or not the shooters were still present to make sure the job was complete, I peered with great caution out of the opening where the driver's side window had been. The coast was clear. *Unbelievable!* I could see the taillights from the very vehicle that carried the people who had just tried to assassinate us as it traveled down the street in the distance as if nothing had happened.

For now, we were safe, and I was free to ask the most grueling question I had to ever ask a person, "Mom! Mom, are you okay?" I yelled. She was crouched motionless, with her head between her legs. The moment of delay sent my heart immediately racing in a panic. The thought of what my life was going to be like without Mom was horrifying. She had been gone so many times before, but never permanently. "Mom!" I yelled again. "Are you okay?" Again no answer. *Those bastards killed my mom!*

Suddenly, she raised her head from her lap, "Oh my God! I can't believe that just happened. I'm all right. What about you?"

Wow! She was okay. She had survived the vile attack as well. That was just like the new Mom God had given me—constantly worrying about others before herself in times of need.

"Caroline, are you all right?" I yelled to the back of the van.

"Yeah, I'm all right," she said looking up from the floor, her face bleeding from the broken glass.

By this time, the whole neighborhood had heard the gunshots and had come outside to try to see who had just been slain in another drive-by shooting. Shaking the broken glass out of my hair and clothes, I stumbled from the van, stunned by the ordeal. *Man, somebody just did a drive-by shooting on us.*

The white minivan was riddled from back to front with bullet holes; much of the metal was shredded. All the windows had been blown out. As I stared at the van in amazement with the crowd of neighbors, my eyes were filled with tears. I knew just how close I had come to that very sudden and unanticipated moment of death. Finally, the police arrived. And the entire incident seemed even more horrific when one of the police officers used tweezers to extract a bullet that had been lodged in the bottom window seal of the driver's door—a bullet that had been intended for me and had landed there when the shooters shot down into the part of the vehicle where I was crouched.

"Man, they shot ya'lls ride all up. Ya'll should be dead," one of the bystanders said in total disbelief.

"Somebody was sho' 'nough looking after ya'll," another person said, shaking her head.

She was exactly right, and at that very moment it hit me. The very God that I had always figured watched over and protected only other people had watched over me during this incident. Not only that, he had been watching over me my entire life—through all my moments of feeling vulnerable, neglected, and unwanted … all the way to the pride and joy I felt at being the first college student in my family.

When I got back to Minnesota a couple days later, still startled and amazed by the fact that I had lived through such an event that could have been so tragic, I made the most important decision I had ever made in my life—the decision to begin my journey to discover the real Tommy Watson. It would be a decision that called for me to spend more time by myself and more time reading the Bible and praying to God. During this time, I began the process of learning to use that painful four-letter word toward myself—a word that had been distorted throughout the course of my life by episodes of pain and disappointment. Nevertheless, for the first time ever, I started to l-o-v-e myself.

My teammates were either amused or found it unbelievable that I had been in a drive-by shooting. Many had heard reports of the shooting in the newspaper; others found out after I was not able to participate in some of the workouts due to strained muscles in my neck from ducking down during the shooting—and probably stress.

"Man, that kind of stuff happens in Colorado?" someone asked. I shrugged and went on preparing for the third season of actually playing football and my fourth year of school … en route for the NFL.

Later that summer, in the midst of my workout, I got a big surprise. I was in motion, in the first stages of a power clean, yanking 300 pounds of weight from the floor. The weight never made it past my knees. I heard and felt a snap, then I found myself doubled over on all fours from the excruciating pain shooting through my lower back.

"Watson, get your ass up and finish the exercise," our strength coach yelled from across the room.

"I can't. I can't even stand up," I said back in fury.

"Well, take your ass upstairs and get some treatment," he said, making his way over to assist another player who was lifting weights.

*Is he blowing me off?* I thought to myself.

I literally dragged myself into the training room. The trainer nonchalantly said, "Go lie down over there and I'll get you some ice." *What the hell? Is that it? Just go lie down over there? I couldn't believe it.* These were the folks that I was supposed to mean so much to. Every painful step revealed to me just how much I really meant to the athletic program of the University of Minnesota.

*But it wasn't supposed to be this way! After all, these are the same people who wined and dined me, and praised me, and told me how happy they were to have me as a part of the team.* That was all nothing more than a myth now that I was hurt. *Surprise, Tommy! Welcome to the other side of sports—the side that is often never talked about.*

Thirty minutes of treatment didn't help the pain at all. How am I going to get back to the dorm in this condition? "Hey, can I get a ride back to the dorm?" I directed my question to one of the trainers who was treating another injured player.

"Tommy, now you know it would be against NCAA rules if I gave you a ride in my car."

"NCAA rules, my ass. I'm hurt and I can't walk or stand up," I snapped back.

"Tommy, I don't make the rules, I just follow the rules," he said walking away.

I couldn't believe it. I didn't know whether to cry in frustration or to attempt to storm into his office and give him a piece of my mind.

Meanwhile, one of my teammates, Big Ray, had been sitting on the table next to me, listening. "Don't worry T-Wat, I got you. I'll carry you back to the dorm." And that he literally did. He helped me off the table and laid me across his shoulders. Lucky for me, Big Ray was one of the stronger and bigger guys on the team

It would be nearly another year before I was able to finally convince the coaches and team doctors to allow me to take an MRI so that I could find out what damage had been done from that weight lifting incident. The test showed that I had herniated disks, pulled ligaments, and a degenerated disk. "Tommy, we're sorry. We didn't think it was that serious," was the response I received from the team doctors.

The best thing to come out of the ordeal was the fact that I was able to walk and work out again about a week after the injury, just in time for my fourth year of sports and school. I had to play through the pain because I was eligible for one more year of school and football because I had been red-shirted as a freshman. This was my chance to get to the NFL. Still not convinced that football was over for me, I prepared myself for the season. And, once again, we finished at the bottom of the Big Ten with a record of 2 and 9. And, once again, I saw only limited playing time on special teams. This was also a season where I found myself having to pay a $200 fee and do a thousand yards of up-downs after I had made an attempt to get my teammates fired up for games against the University of Michigan and the University of Iowa—an attempt that had caused broken mirrors in two locker rooms.

The light in my head was starting to shine to a different bulb—a bulb that told me my future might not be with football. So I decided, on a whim, to see my academic advisor to determine if there was any possibility I might get my degree.

Ms. Lucas, my program advisor in the College of Human Ecology, simply shook her head as she looked over my grades and the number of classes I would need to graduate.

"Well, is there anything we can do?" I asked, breaking the silence.

"It would be a very long shot for you to be able to graduate with the credits and classes you need before your scholarship expires," she said, looking over the top of her glasses.

"Whatever it takes, I'm willing to do it." I slid up to the edge of my chair. "Can you help me put together a plan for every class I need to take and tell me every grade I need to get in order to graduate?"

"I can, but I don't know how you're going to accomplish this task, with football and the fact that you waited until the end of college to take all your tough classes."

I left her office that day looking at the nearly impossible schedule that I was going to have to follow, shaking my head in disgust. How was I going to accomplish the monumental task of graduating from college? The fact that most athletes never graduated from college was not a statistic that worked in my favor. I had nothing to return to back home in Denver.

But still, I had my final season of football ahead of me where anything to do with going to the NFL was possible.

My involvement with a campus group called Athletes in Action, a student-focused Christian group, had opened up doors for me to hear speakers like former Minnesota Vikings greats Jeff Seamen and Chris Carter. I was both amazed and shocked hearing them share stories from the past and where they had come from.

Man, I would be too embarrassed to stand in front of anyone and tell them stuff like that about me, I thought, when I heard Chris Carter talk about his addiction to drugs and what his life had been like when he was growing up in the projects with his mom and no dad. And yet, the more and more I heard stories like this, the more I started to become inspired to explore the idea of sharing my own story.

And that opportunity soon followed. After months of agonizing over what people would think, I decided to share publicly for the first time my situation growing up. During a fifteen-minute, knee-shaking speech I delivered at the Harriet Tubman Center in Minneapolis, a battered women's shelter for women and kids, I told my story. This was an event I had taken the liberty of setting up for the entire team and coaches. At the end of the grueling speech, the tears of joy from the mothers and the glowing smiles on the faces of the kids "wowed" me.

"Thank you, brother, for sharing your story," one of the mothers told me. "You are a testimony for me and my kids. We can make it through these tough times." Other mothers thanked me as well.

I was blown away by the fact that something that had always brought me pain and embarrassment had brought inspiration to others.

Even though we came from two different worlds, we shared a very common theme in our lives—a theme of pain, hurt, and neglect. But still, I didn't realize the magnitude of what I had shared that day.

My second opportunity to share my story publicly came in the July 16, 1996, Sunday edition of the St. Paul Pioneer Press newspaper. The front page of the sports section featured a picture and article about the retirement of the legendary Kirby Puckett from the Minnesota Twins. But, at the bottom of the page, was a picture of me and an article entitled "Dodging a Bullet." My story was originally supposed to be a small article that would run in Tuesday's edition in the metro section of the paper, which would have been fine with me. But my interview with sports writer Bob Sansevere, originally scheduled for half an hour, had run for nearly an hour. "Tommy, I'm going to send a photographer over to you right away so we can get a picture of you to run with the article in tomorrow's newspaper." Bob Sansevere did a great job laying out in detail my life growing up in Denver. I had no idea how the public would receive it.

My answering machine was filled with messages the entire day. The messages from friends ranged from sadness to anger.

"Man, Tommy, I had no idea that you had to live like that." "How in the world could you share something like that with the newspaper? Don't you know you shouldn't be putting all your business out in the streets like that?" But still I didn't understand the magnitude of what I was sharing. And life went on.

Meanwhile, with my last and final season in progress, I decided that I was going to take certain classes that interfered with my football schedule. This was something that didn't sit well with my coach.

"Don't you know missing practice like this is going to cost you a lot of your playing time?" Coach Smith asked me during our one-on-one meeting in his office. "You are a senior."

"I'm sure it will," I responded, shrugging my shoulders. *My playing time hasn't changed in any of the years before this; why should it change now?*

Our first game of the season landed us in Monroe, Louisiana, to play the North East Louisiana Raging Cajuns. The signs all around town and throughout the newspapers read, "Big Time Comes to Town."

Upon our arrival to the stadium just before the game, the smell of fresh smoked barbecue filled the hot, humid, mosquito-infested night air. Music whistled throughout the parking lot from the cars of the thousands of fans who were tailgating in the parking lot, many of whom were indulging in alcoholic beverages.

"Them wild Cajuns down there are going to be like nothing you have ever seen before," our coach warned us before our arrival at Monroe. And he was right; this had to be the closest thing to Mardi Gras I had ever seen. People danced around, hooting and hollering. *Man, I thought, all of this just for a football game. These got to be some of the best fans in the country.* That was a statement that held true all through the game as we crushed their Raging Cajun football team. That Raging Cajun crowd of 3600 displayed more excitement than some of those monstrous Big Ten crowds we'd played against! As players, we had felt their energy.

After this game, I began to detach myself emotionally from the game of football. My plan was to just go through the motions until the final game of the season was upon me and I could walk away from the sport and not look back. But, my career ended more prematurely than I had expected during the third game of the season against Donovan McNabb and the Syracuse Orangeman, when the pain from my back injury became unbearable from the strenuous physical activity entailed in playing football.

My decision to stop playing was followed by a night of nonstop and unexpected bout of tears and sadness. I never thought it would be so difficult to end my relationship with the game of football, but it was the right time for me to gracefully bow out. The marriage was over.

The newspaper the day following my decision read, "U of M Running Back Sees Career Degenerated."

Even more shocking than seeing my decision to stop playing in the headlines was this statement from my position coach, "When Tommy graduates at the end of the school year, it will be an unbelievable achievement for someone who grew up in the circumstances he did. He'll be one of the all-time success stories in the history of Minnesota, given his background and all the hardships."

Wow. The very fact that he would mention my name with the words "graduation" and "unbelievable achievement" sparked a fire in me to try even harder to make the grades I needed for graduation.

But I still didn't understand why so many people seemed interested in hearing my story.

Shortly after my decision to stop playing football, another article about my story appeared. The headline ran, "Watson shows heroism has many forms." The article went on to say, "Watson is proof that no matter how much emotional sludge and misery life hurls at you, you can dust yourself off and keep going." These words were followed by a quote that would have never come from my mouth prior to my sports injury, "A lot of kids think their only way out is by becoming a pro athlete. I tell them you can still be someone without going to the NFL or NBA."

A few weeks later, Channel 11 News ran a special about my life growing up in Denver. "Tonight you're going to meet a young man who survived insurmountable obstacles in one of Denver's toughest neighborhoods," were the words that opened up the special. "Tommy Watson's story is both inspiring and gutsy."

*Why would my story mean anything to anyone?*

Shortly after this special aired, I was cruising through the mall looking for shoes when a young African American male I had never seen before stopped and gave me a big hug. *What in the hell is wrong with this dude?* I waited for a response from the young man whose eyes were now filled with tears.

"Man, thanks for telling your story. Me and you have a lot in common. And one day I'm going to go around doing the same thing you're doing," he said. He walked off and left me dumbfounded. *What is it that I am doing?* All I had done was share events of my life.

Even though I had quit playing football, I still came around to show support for my teammates. One day, as I was walking through the hallway on my way to watch practice, one of the coaches said to me in passing, "Congratulations on being one of the 'Big Ten People You Should Know.'"

I later discovered that he was talking about the Big Ten conference homepage for Big Ten athletes who had reached difficult achievements. The article read, "The game against Syracuse may have marked the end of Tommy Watson's career, but not the end of his impact on players, teammates, and anyone else who meets him." Very interesting, especially since I had never thought of myself having an impact on my teammates, or on anyone else around me.

The end of the football season and my career with football coincided with the end of the NCAA rule that prohibited student-athletes from working during the academic year; supposedly we would be receiving extra benefits we might have been able to earn had we been able to work prior to this moment.

My first job as an intern landed me at St. Paul Public Housing Agency as a rental technician. My job was to assist the other rental technicians in maintaining a 99 percent occupancy rate each month in the public housing apartments the city owned. Maintaining this extraordinary rental rate didn't even put a dent in the city's poverty and homelessness statistics, which reflected mostly women and kids.

Families came in day after day, fleeing from domestic abuse and slumlords, and we could offer them only a chance to be on our waiting list for six months to a year. It was very tough emotionally on them—as well as on us.

"Sir, we have nowhere else to go," one mother said, holding an infant in one arm, a toddler in the other, and telling three others to get off my desk.

After dealing with situations like this, I'd go off to a grueling day of class. I was hanging on by my fingernails in very difficult classes—drafting, economics, and physics. I had learned by my senior year to seek extra help from my professors, so, when I wasn't in class, I was usually in one of my professors' offices, trying to make sense of all the material that I didn't understand, which was most of it.

Back at the dorm, in my new bachelor's pad, it was phone off, curtains shut, and door locked to keep out every distraction. There was no more going to the lakes and hanging out with the fellas. "T-Wat, what's up with you? You don't even hang out no more," I heard as I dropped briefly into the lunchroom one day for dinner before heading back to my room.

The days of dating astronomical numbers of women were no more.

Keeping my curtains closed kept me from the temptation of the beautiful spring sunshine—always a big deal in cold Minnesota. I had to stay focused.

One weekend while I was taking a break, I received a phone call from one of my former coaches and mentors. He wanted to talk to me about a conversation that he and I had had months earlier, when we had discussed the idea of a book about my life.

"Tommy, I talked with a few people I know about the book thing, and I'm sad to tell you that many of them felt that people wouldn't really be interested in reading a book like yours," he said gently.

"Is that right?" I responded, slamming down my books and hanging up the phone.

The more I pursued this idea, the more farfetched it seemed. Maybe my story was just a good story for the newspapers. This idea was reinforced even more one day after I mentioned the book idea to a couple of my close teammates.

"Man, are you crazy? Don't nobody want to read no book about yo' life. I think you losing yo' mind. The next thing you'll be talking about is some dumb movie about yo' life," one of them said, falling to the floor in laughter and creating a tidal wave of laughter among the others.

As I walked away, my eyes filled with tears. *What if I'd never persevered through the foster homes? What if I'd never persevered through the crisis centers? What if I'd never persevered through the motel rooms? What if I'd never persevered through my parents' many years of incarceration? What if I'd never persevered through failed expectations of teachers? What if I'd never persevered through the pain of having family tell me I would never be anything or achieve anything in life? ... through the ridicule of my peers? ... through the disappointment of having many family members die of alcohol and drugs? ... through the strain of stepping out of my comfort zone into a place like Mullen High school? ... through the terror of nearly being homeless? ... through depression and suicidal thoughts? What if I'd never persevered through the shocking revelation that I would not be playing in the NFL one day? What if? What if?*

Well, the reality of it all is this: had I not persevered through these many painful episodes of my life that often seemed hopeless, I would not have been standing where I was on one particular day—that special day in 1997 when I became the first person in my family to attend—and now graduate—from college. Wow! What a proud moment it was for me, with my new theme song, Mariah Carey's "Hero," playing in the background as I crossed the stage to receive my college degree.

In the words of my good friend Jamil Salaam, "Often, during troubled and chaotic times, miracles are born."

*No matter what your situation may be or may look like, hold on, you can make it. You can persevere, and life will go on.*

Today, Tommy Watson resides in Minnesota. He is happily married to the love of his life, Akesha. In addition, he considers himself the luckiest father in the world to have two brilliant sons (Martice and Avery) and two princesses for daughters (Darien and Torri).

Tommy is a principal in the Minnesota public school system. He received a Bachelor of Science from the University of Minnesota; a Masters in Educational Administration; and an advanced graduate degree in K-12 administration. He is currently working on his doctor of Education degree.

Tommy also is a motivational speaker and consultant. Feel to contact him at the information listed below.

Reach One Communications
P.O. Box 43022
Brooklyn Park, MN 55443
Tommywatson32@yahoo.com
www.reachonecommunications.com

# *Final Thoughts from the Author*

First of all, thank you to my Lord and Savior Jesus Christ for
allowing me to make it through such a difficult past.

Thank you to my wife and kids for your support during this
nearly ten-year book writing process.

Thank you to the multitude of family members and friends who supported
me
throughout my life, throughout all of my story.

And, a special thank you to Oprah Winfrey, whose soulful interviews with
wonderful and amazing people inspired me to make two major decisions
in my adulthood. The first decision was to write this book. The second
decision was to become a school principal. Both decisions have brought me
immeasurable growth and happiness.
I hope we get a chance to meet someday.

The people who have provided me assistance over the years with A Face of
Courage
are too numerous to list. You know who you are. Thank you and God bless.

Until we meet again … take care.